MznLnx

Missing Links Exam Preps

Exam Prep for

Linear Algebra

Friedberg & Insel & Spence, 4th Edition

The MznLnx Exam Prep is your link from the texbook and lecture to your exams.
The MznLnx Exam Preps are unauthorized and comprehensive reviews of your textbooks.

All material provided by MznLnx and Rico Publications (c) 2010
Textbook publishers and textbook authors do not particpate in or contribute to these reviews.

MznLnx

Rico Publications

Exam Prep for Linear Algebra
4th Edition
Friedberg & Insel & Spence

Publisher: Raymond Houge
Assistant Editor: Michael Rouger
Text and Cover Designer: Lisa Buckner
Marketing Manager: Sara Swagger
Project Manager, Editorial Production: Jerry Emerson
Art Director: Vernon Lowerui

Product Manager: Dave Mason
Editorial Assitant: Rachel Guzmanji
Pedagogy: Debra Long
Cover Image: Jim Reed/Getty Images
Text and Cover Printer: City Printing, Inc.
Compositor: Media Mix, Inc.

(c) 2010 Rico Publications
ALL RIGHTS RESERVED. No part of this work covered by the copyright may be reproduced or used in any form or by an means--graphic, electronic, or mechanical, including photocopying, recording, taping, Web distribution, information storage, and retrieval systems, or in any other manner--without the written permission of the publisher.

Printed in the United States
ISBN:

For more information about our products, contact us at:
Dave.Mason@RicoPublications.com

For permission to use material from this text or product, submit a request online to:
Dave.Mason@RicoPublications.com

Contents

CHAPTER 1
Vector Spaces   1

CHAPTER 2
Linear Transformations and Matrices   25

CHAPTER 3
Elementary Matrix Operations and Systems of Linear Equations   51

CHAPTER 4
Determinants of Order   66

CHAPTER 5
Eigenvalues and Eigenvectors   80

CHAPTER 6
Inner Product Spaces   104

CHAPTER 7
Canonical Forms   142

ANSWER KEY   160

TO THE STUDENT

COMPREHENSIVE

The *MznLnx* Exam Prep series is designed to help you pass your exams. Editors at MznLnx review your textbooks and then prepare these practice exams to help you master the textbook material. Unlike study guides, workbooks, and practice tests provided by the texbook publisher and textbook authors, *MznLnx* gives you **all** of the material in each chapter in exam form, not just samples, so you can be sure to nail your exam.

MECHANICAL

The MznLnx Exam Prep series creates exams that will help you learn the subject matter as well as test you on your understanding. Each question is designed to help you master the concept. Just working through the exams, you gain an understanding of the subject--its a simple mechanical process that produces success.

INTEGRATED STUDY GUIDE AND REVIEW

MznLnx is not just a set of exams designed to test you, its also a comprehensive review of the subject content. Each exam question is also a review of the concept, making sure that you will get the answer correct without having to go to other sources of material. You learn as you go! Its the easiest way to pass an exam.

HUMOR

Studying can be tedious and dry. MznLnx's instructional design includes moderate humor within the exam questions on occassion, to break the tedium and revitalize the brain

Chapter 1. Vector Spaces

1. In physics and in _____ calculus, a spatial _____, or simply _____, is a concept characterized by a magnitude and a direction.
   a. Vector0
   b. Thing
   c. Undefined
   d. Undefined

2. _____ is a collection of objects called vectors that, informally speaking, may be scaled and added.
   a. Vector space0
   b. Thing
   c. Undefined
   d. Undefined

3. _____ of an object is its speed in a particular direction.
   a. Velocity0
   b. Thing
   c. Undefined
   d. Undefined

4. _____ is a set, with some particular properties and usually some additional structure, such as the operations of addition or multiplication, for instance.
   a. Space0
   b. Thing
   c. Undefined
   d. Undefined

5. A _____ is a set whose members are members of another set or a set contained within another set.
   a. Subset0
   b. Thing
   c. Undefined
   d. Undefined

6. _____ are groups whose members are members of another set or a set contained within another set.

Chapter 1. Vector Spaces

   a. Thing
   b. Subsets0
   c. Undefined
   d. Undefined

7. In combinatorial mathematics, a _____ is an un-ordered collection of unique elements.
   a. Combination0
   b. Concept
   c. Undefined
   d. Undefined

8. The word _____ comes from the Latin word linearis, which means created by lines.
   a. Linear0
   b. Thing
   c. Undefined
   d. Undefined

9. A _____ is an equation in which each term is either a constant or the product of a constant times the first power of a variable.
   a. Linear equation0
   b. Thing
   c. Undefined
   d. Undefined

10. The _____ of a mathematical object is its size: a property by which it can be larger or smaller than other objects of the same kind; in technical terms, an ordering of the class of objects to which it belongs.
    a. Magnitude0
    b. Thing
    c. Undefined
    d. Undefined

11. _____ is a kind of property which exists as magnitude or multitude. It is among the basic classes of things along with quality, substance, change, and relation.

a. Amount0
b. Thing
c. Undefined
d. Undefined

12. In physics, _____ is an influence that may cause an object to accelerate. It may be experienced as a lift, a push, or a pull. The actual acceleration of the body is determined by the vector sum of all forces acting on it, known as net _____ or resultant _____.
a. Thing
b. Force0
c. Undefined
d. Undefined

13. _____ is defined as the rate of change or derivative with respect to time of velocity.
a. Acceleration0
b. Thing
c. Undefined
d. Undefined

14. A _____ is the result of the addition of a set of numbers. The numbers may be natural numbers, complex numbers, matrices, or still more complicated objects. An infinite _____ is a subtle procedure known as a series.
a. Sum0
b. Thing
c. Undefined
d. Undefined

15. A _____ is a special kind of ratio, indicating a relationship between two measurements with different units, such as miles to gallons or cents to pounds.
a. Rate0
b. Thing
c. Undefined
d. Undefined

16. A _____ is a unit of length, usually used to measure distance, in a number of different systems, including Imperial units, United States customary units and Norwegian/Swedish mil. Its size can vary from system to system, but in each is between 1 and 10 kilometers. In contemporary English contexts _____ refers to either:

Chapter 1. Vector Spaces

a. Mile0
b. Thing
c. Undefined
d. Undefined

17. _____ is a unit of speed, expressing the number of international miles covered per hour.
   a. Thing
   b. Miles per hour0
   c. Undefined
   d. Undefined

18. In the scientific method, an _____ (Latin: ex-+-periri, "of (or from) trying"), is a set of actions and observations, performed in the context of solving a particular problem or question, in order to support or falsify a hypothesis or research concerning phenomena.
   a. Thing
   b. Experiment0
   c. Undefined
   d. Undefined

19. A _____ is a four-sided plane figure that has two sets of opposite parallel sides.
   a. Concept
   b. Parallelogram0
   c. Undefined
   d. Undefined

20. A _____ can refer to a line joining two nonadjacent vertices of a polygon or polyhedron, or in some contexts any upward or downward sloping line. .
   a. Diagonal0
   b. Thing
   c. Undefined
   d. Undefined

21. In geometry, _____ angles are angles that have a common ray coming out of the vertex going between two other rays.

a. Concept
b. Adjacent0
c. Undefined
d. Undefined

22. In geometry, an _____ is a point at which a line segment or ray terminates.
   a. Endpoint0
   b. Thing
   c. Undefined
   d. Undefined

23. In mathematics, the additive inverse, or _____ of a number n is the number that, when added to n, yields zero. The additive inverse of n is denoted −n. For example, 7 is −7, because 7 + (−7) = 0, and the additive inverse of −0.3 is 0.3, because −0.3 + 0.3 = 0.
   a. Opposite0
   b. Thing
   c. Undefined
   d. Undefined

24. In mathematics, the _____ of a number n is the number that, when added to n, yields zero. The _____ of n is denoted −n. For example, 7 is −7, because 7 + (−7) = 0, and the _____ of −0.3 is 0.3, because −0.3 + 0.3 = 0.
   a. Additive inverse0
   b. Thing
   c. Undefined
   d. Undefined

25. _____ is the study of geometry using the principles of algebra. _____ can be explained more simply: it is concerned with defining geometrical shapes in a numerical way and extracting numerical information from that representation.
   a. Thing
   b. Analytic geometry0
   c. Undefined
   d. Undefined

26. A _____ is a set of numbers that designate location in a given reference system, such as x,y in a planar _____ system or an x,y,z in a three-dimensional _____ system.

Chapter 1. Vector Spaces

  a. Coordinate0
  b. Thing
  c. Undefined
  d. Undefined

27. In mathematics and its applications, a _____ is a system for assigning an n-tuple of numbers or scalars to each point in an n-dimensional space.
  a. Concept
  b. Coordinate system0
  c. Undefined
  d. Undefined

28. In mathematics, the _____ of a coordinate system is the point where the axes of the system intersect.
  a. Thing
  b. Origin0
  c. Undefined
  d. Undefined

29. In mathematics, a _____ is a two-dimensional manifold or surface that is perfectly flat.
  a. Thing
  b. Plane0
  c. Undefined
  d. Undefined

30. In mathematics, a _____ may be described informally as a number that can be given by an infinite decimal representation.
  a. Real number0
  b. Thing
  c. Undefined
  d. Undefined

31. In mathematics, _____ is an elementary arithmetic operation. When one of the numbers is a whole number, _____ is the repeated sum of the other number.

a. Multiplication0
b. Thing
c. Undefined
d. Undefined

32. In linear algebra, real numbers are called scalars and relate to vectors in a vector space through the operation of _____ multiplication, in which a vector can be multiplied by a number to produce another vector.
a. Thing
b. Scalar0
c. Undefined
d. Undefined

33. _____ is one of the basic operations defining a vector space in linear algebra.
a. Thing
b. Scalar multiplication0
c. Undefined
d. Undefined

34. In mathematics, science including computer science, linguistics and engineering, an _____ is, generally speaking, an independent variable or input to a function.
a. Thing
b. Argument0
c. Undefined
d. Undefined

35. A _____ of a number is the product of that number with any integer.
a. Multiple0
b. Thing
c. Undefined
d. Undefined

36. A _____ decimal is a decimal fraction which ends after a definite number of digits.

Chapter 1. Vector Spaces

   a. Thing
   b. Terminating0
   c. Undefined
   d. Undefined

37. In mathematics, the _____ of two sets A and B is the set that contains all elements of A that also belong to B (or equivalently, all elements of B that also belong to A), but no other elements.
   a. Intersection0
   b. Thing
   c. Undefined
   d. Undefined

38. In geometry, a line _____ is a part of a line that is bounded by two end points, and contains every point on the line between its end points.
   a. Segment0
   b. Concept
   c. Undefined
   d. Undefined

39. A _____ is a part of a line that is bounded by two end points, and contains every point on the line between its end points.
   a. Line segment0
   b. Thing
   c. Undefined
   d. Undefined

40. _____ is the middle point of a line segment.
   a. Midpoint0
   b. Thing
   c. Undefined
   d. Undefined

41. An _____ or member of a set is an object that when collected together make up the set.

a. Element0
b. Thing
c. Undefined
d. Undefined

42. The _____ is a rule which states that when you add or multiply numbers, changing the order doesn't change the result.
   a. Commutative law0
   b. Thing
   c. Undefined
   d. Undefined

43. In mathematics, _____ is a property that a binary operation can have. Within an expression containing two or more of the same associative operators in a row, the order of operations does not matter as long as the sequence of the operands is not changed.
   a. Thing
   b. Associativity0
   c. Undefined
   d. Undefined

44. In mathematics, the _____ , or members of a set or more generally a class are all those objects which when collected together make up the set or class.
   a. Thing
   b. Elements0
   c. Undefined
   d. Undefined

45. In mathematics, a _____ is the result of multiplying, or an expression that identifies factors to be multiplied.
   a. Product0
   b. Thing
   c. Undefined
   d. Undefined

46. In mathematics, in the field of group theory, a _____ of a group is a quasisimple subnormal subgroup.

Chapter 1. Vector Spaces

  a. Concept
  b. Component0
  c. Undefined
  d. Undefined

47. In mathematics, a matrix can be thought of as each row or _____ being a vector. Hence, a space formed by row vectors or _____ vectors are said to be a row space or a _____ space.
  a. Column0
  b. Concept
  c. Undefined
  d. Undefined

48. In mathematics, a _____ is a rectangular table of numbers or, more generally, a table consisting of abstract quantities that can be added and multiplied.
  a. Matrix0
  b. Thing
  c. Undefined
  d. Undefined

49. The _____ integers are all the integers from zero on upwards.
  a. Thing
  b. Nonnegative0
  c. Undefined
  d. Undefined

50. In mathematics, a _____ is a constant multiplicative factor of a certain object. The object can be such things as a variable, a vector, a function, etc. For example, the _____ of $9x^2$ is 9.
  a. Thing
  b. Coefficient0
  c. Undefined
  d. Undefined

51. An _____ is a combination of numbers, operators, grouping symbols and/or free variables and bound variables arranged in a meaningful way which can be evaluated..

Chapter 1. Vector Spaces

a. Thing
b. Expression0
c. Undefined
d. Undefined

52. In mathematics, there are several meanings of _____ depending on the subject.
a. Degree0
b. Thing
c. Undefined
d. Undefined

53. In mathematics, a _____ is an expression that is constructed from one or more variables and constants, using only the operations of addition, subtraction, multiplication, and constant positive whole number exponents. is a _____. Note in particular that division by an expression containing a variable is not in general allowed in polynomials. [1]
a. Thing
b. Polynomial0
c. Undefined
d. Undefined

54. The _____ is the maximum of the degrees of all terms in the polynomial.
a. Degree of a polynomial0
b. Thing
c. Undefined
d. Undefined

55. Mathematical _____ is used to represent ideas.
a. Notation0
b. Thing
c. Undefined
d. Undefined

56. The mathematical concept of a _____ expresses the intuitive idea of deterministic dependence between two quantities, one of which is viewed as primary and the other as secondary. A _____ then is a way to associate a unique output for each input of a specified type, for example, a real number or an element of a given set.

a. Thing
b. Function0
c. Undefined
d. Undefined

57. In mathematics, a _____ is an ordered list of objects. Like a set, it contains members, also called elements or terms, and the number of terms is called the length of the _____. Unlike a set, order matters, and the exact same elements can appear multiple times at different positions in the _____.
a. Thing
b. Sequence0
c. Undefined
d. Undefined

58. In mathematics, a set is called _____ if there is a bijection between the set and some set of the form {1, 2, ..., n} where n is a natural number.
a. Thing
b. Finite0
c. Undefined
d. Undefined

59. In mathematics, a _____ is a statement that can be proved on the basis of explicitly stated or previously agreed assumptions.
a. Theorem0
b. Thing
c. Undefined
d. Undefined

60. In mathematics, the notion of _____ is a generalization of the notion of invertible.
a. Thing
b. Cancellation0
c. Undefined
d. Undefined

61. In linear algebra and related areas of mathematics, the null vector or _____ is the vector in Euclidean space, all of whose components are zero.

Chapter 1. Vector Spaces

   a. Zero vector0
   b. Thing
   c. Undefined
   d. Undefined

62. _____ element of an element x with respect to a binary operation * with identity element e is an element y such that x * y = y * x = e. In particular,
   a. Thing
   b. Inverse0
   c. Undefined
   d. Undefined

63. In mathematics, the _____ inverse, or opposite, of a number n is the number that, when added to n, yields zero. The _____ inverse of n is denoted −n.
   a. Thing
   b. Additive0
   c. Undefined
   d. Undefined

64. A _____ is a mathematical statement which follows easily from a previously proven statement, typically a mathematical theorem.
   a. Corollary0
   b. Thing
   c. Undefined
   d. Undefined

65. The _____ is a measurement of how a function changes when the values of its inputs change.
   a. Derivative0
   b. Thing
   c. Undefined
   d. Undefined

66. _____ are functions which satisfy particular symmetry relations, with respect to taking additive inverses.

Chapter 1. Vector Spaces

   a. Even function0
   b. Thing
   c. Undefined
   d. Undefined

67. In mathematics, _____ and odd functions are functions which satisfy particular symmetry relations, with respect to taking additive inverses.
   a. Even functions0
   b. Thing
   c. Undefined
   d. Undefined

68. An _____ is a collection of two not necessarily distinct objects, one of which is distinguished as the first coordinate and the other as the second coordinate.
   a. Thing
   b. Ordered pair0
   c. Undefined
   d. Undefined

69. In mathematics, the conjugate _____ or adjoint matrix of an m-by-n matrix A with complex entries is the n-by-m matrix A* obtained from A by taking the transpose and then taking the complex conjugate of each entry.
   a. Thing
   b. Pairs0
   c. Undefined
   d. Undefined

70. In mathematics, a _____ number is a number which can be expressed as a ratio of two integers. Non-integer _____ numbers (commonly called fractions) are usually written as the vulgar fraction a / b, where b is not zero.
   a. Rational0
   b. Thing
   c. Undefined
   d. Undefined

71. In linear algebra, the _____ of a matrix A is another matrix AT

Chapter 1. Vector Spaces 15

　a. Thing
　b. Transpose0
　c. Undefined
　d. Undefined

72. In mathematics, particularly linear algebra, a _____ is a matrix with all its entries being zero.
　a. Thing
　b. Zero matrix0
　c. Undefined
　d. Undefined

73. A _____ function is a function for which, intuitively, small changes in the input result in small changes in the output.
　a. Continuous0
　b. Event
　c. Undefined
　d. Undefined

74. In mathematics and the mathematical sciences, a _____ is a fixed, but possibly unspecified, value. This is in contrast to a variable, which is not fixed.
　a. Constant0
　b. Thing
　c. Undefined
　d. Undefined

75. _____ is a function whose values do not vary and thus are constant.
　a. Constant function0
　b. Thing
　c. Undefined
　d. Undefined

76. _____ is a square matrix in which the entries outside the main diagonal are all zero.

16 *Chapter 1. Vector Spaces*

   a. Diagonal matrix0
   b. Thing
   c. Undefined
   d. Undefined

77. In linear algebra, the _____ of an n-by-n square matrix A is defined to be the sum of the elements on the main diagonal of A,
   a. Trace0
   b. Thing
   c. Undefined
   d. Undefined

78. In mathematics, a _____ is a demonstration that, assuming certain axioms, some statement is necessarily true.
   a. Proof0
   b. Thing
   c. Undefined
   d. Undefined

79. In mathematics and more specifically set theory, the _____ set is the unique set which contains no elements.
   a. Thing
   b. Empty0
   c. Undefined
   d. Undefined

80. In plane geometry, a _____ is a polygon with four equal sides, four right angles, and parallel opposite sides. In algebra, the _____ of a number is that number multiplied by itself.
   a. Square0
   b. Thing
   c. Undefined
   d. Undefined

81. In mathematics, _____ describes an entity with a limit.

Chapter 1. Vector Spaces

   a. Thing
   b. Convergent0
   c. Undefined
   d. Undefined

82. The _____, the average in everyday English, which is also called the arithmetic _____ (and is distinguished from the geometric _____ or harmonic _____). The average is also called the sample _____. The expected value of a random variable, which is also called the population _____.
   a. Thing
   b. Mean0
   c. Undefined
   d. Undefined

83. In mathematics and logic, a _____ proof is a way of showing the truth or falsehood of a given statement by a straightforward combination of established facts, usually existing lemmas and theorems, without making any further assumptions.
   a. Direct0
   b. Thing
   c. Undefined
   d. Undefined

84. The _____ of a ring R is defined to be the smallest positive integer n such that $n\,a = 0$, for all a in R.
   a. Characteristic0
   b. Thing
   c. Undefined
   d. Undefined

85. In mathematics, if G is a group, H a subgroup of G, and g an element of G, then, gH = {gh : h an element of H } is a left _____ of H in G, and Hg = {hg : h an element of H } is a right _____ of H in G.
   a. Thing
   b. Coset0
   c. Undefined
   d. Undefined

86. In mathematics, a _____ is the end result of a division problem. It can also be expressed as the number of times the divisor divides into the dividend.

Chapter 1. Vector Spaces

   a. Thing
   b. Quotient0
   c. Undefined
   d. Undefined

87. _____ traditionally refers to the statistical process of determining comparable scores on different forms of an exam
   a. Thing
   b. Equating0
   c. Undefined
   d. Undefined

88. A _____ is a number, figure, or indicator that appears below the normal line of type, typically used in a formula, mathematical expression, or description of a chemical compound.
   a. Subscript0
   b. Thing
   c. Undefined
   d. Undefined

89. _____ Logic is a concept in traditional logic referring to a "type of immediate inference in which from a given proposition another proposition is inferred which has as its subject the predicate of the original proposition and as its predicate the subject of the original proposition (the quality of the proposition being retained)."
   a. Concept
   b. Converse0
   c. Undefined
   d. Undefined

90. In common philosophical language, a proposition or _____, is the content of an assertion, that is, it is true-or-false and defined by the meaning of a particular piece of language.
   a. Statement0
   b. Concept
   c. Undefined
   d. Undefined

91. _____ the expected value of a random variable displays the average or central value of the variable. It is a summary value of the distribution of the variable.

a. Determining0
b. Thing
c. Undefined
d. Undefined

92. In mathematics, a _____ occurs if there is a bijection between the set and some set of the form 1, 2, ..., n where n is a natural number.
a. Finite set0
b. Concept
c. Undefined
d. Undefined

93. _____ is a special kind of square matrix where the entries below or above the main diagonal are zero.
a. Triangular form0
b. Thing
c. Undefined
d. Undefined

94. A _____ fraction is a fraction in which the absolute value of the numerator is less than the denominator--hence, the absolute value of the fraction is less than 1.
a. Proper0
b. Thing
c. Undefined
d. Undefined

95. _____ also called natural basis or canonical basis of the n-dimensional Euclidean space Rn is the basis obtained by taking the n basis vectors
a. Thing
b. Standard basis0
c. Undefined
d. Undefined

96. Mathematical _____ are the wide variety of ways to capture an abstract mathematical concept or relationship.

Chapter 1. Vector Spaces

a. Thing
b. Representations0
c. Undefined
d. Undefined

97. A _____ is a deliberate process for transforming one or more inputs into one or more results.
a. Thing
b. Calculation0
c. Undefined
d. Undefined

98. A _____ consists either of a suggested explanation for a phenomenon or of a reasoned proposal suggesting a possible correlation between multiple phenomena.
a. Hypothesis0
b. Thing
c. Undefined
d. Undefined

99. _____ is the state of being greater than any finite real or natural number, however large.
a. Thing
b. Infinite0
c. Undefined
d. Undefined

100. _____ is the study of terms and their use — of words and compound words that are used in specific contexts.
a. Thing
b. Terminology0
c. Undefined
d. Undefined

101. In a mathematical proof or a syllogism, a _____ is a statement that is the logical consequence of preceding statements.

a. Concept
b. Conclusion0
c. Undefined
d. Undefined

102. An _____ in policy debate is part of a speech which is flagged as not responding to the line-by-line arguments on the flow.
a. Overview0
b. Thing
c. Undefined
d. Undefined

103. A _____ is an illustration used in the branch of mathematics known as set theory. It shows all of the possible mathematical or logical relationships between sets.
a. Venn diagram0
b. Thing
c. Undefined
d. Undefined

104. A _____ is a simplified and structured visual representation of concepts, ideas, constructions, relations, statistical data, anatomy etc used in all aspects of human activities to visualize and clarify the topic.
a. Diagram0
b. Thing
c. Undefined
d. Undefined

105. _____ is a method of constructing new data points from a discrete set of known data points.
a. Thing
b. Interpolation0
c. Undefined
d. Undefined

106. In numerical analysis, a _____, named after Joseph Louis Lagrange, is the interpolation polynomial for a given set of data points in the Lagrange form.

a. Lagrange polynomial0
b. Thing
c. Undefined
d. Undefined

107. A _____ signifies a point or points of probability on a subject e.g., the _____ of creativity, which allows for the formation of rule or norm or law by interpretation of the phenomena events that can be created.
a. Principle0
b. Thing
c. Undefined
d. Undefined

108. In set theory and other branches of mathematics, the _____ of a collection of sets is the set that contains everything that belongs to any of the sets, but nothing else.
a. Thing
b. Union0
c. Undefined
d. Undefined

109. _____ has many meanings, most of which simply .
a. Thing
b. Power0
c. Undefined
d. Undefined

110. In mathematics, two sets are said to be _____ if they have no element in common. For example, {1, 2, 3} and {4, 5, 6} are sets which are _____.
a. Disjoint0
b. Thing
c. Undefined
d. Undefined

111. Equivalence is the condition of being _____ or essentially equal.

a. Equivalent0
b. Thing
c. Undefined
d. Undefined

112. An _____ is any starting assumption from which other statements are logically derived
a. Axiom0
b. Thing
c. Undefined
d. Undefined

113. In logic, statements p and q are _____ if they have the same logical content.
a. Thing
b. Logically equivalent0
c. Undefined
d. Undefined

114. In mathematics, a _____ is a countable collection of open covers of a topological space that satisfies certain separation axioms.
a. Development0
b. Thing
c. Undefined
d. Undefined

115. _____ is a branch of mathematics concerning the study of structure, relation and quantity.
a. Algebra0
b. Concept
c. Undefined
d. Undefined

116. In mathematics, a _____ number is a real or complex number which is not algebraic, that is, not a solution of a non-zero polynomial equation, with rational coefficients.

a. Thing
b. Transcendental0
c. Undefined
d. Undefined

Chapter 2. Linear Transformations and Matrices

1. In mathematics, a _____ in elementary terms is any of a variety of different functions from geometry, such as rotations, reflections and translations.
   a. Thing
   b. Transformation0
   c. Undefined
   d. Undefined

2. In mathematics, _____ is an elementary arithmetic operation. When one of the numbers is a whole number, _____ is the repeated sum of the other number.
   a. Multiplication0
   b. Thing
   c. Undefined
   d. Undefined

3. In physics and in _____ calculus, a spatial _____, or simply _____, is a concept characterized by a magnitude and a direction.
   a. Thing
   b. Vector0
   c. Undefined
   d. Undefined

4. _____ is a collection of objects called vectors that, informally speaking, may be scaled and added.
   a. Thing
   b. Vector space0
   c. Undefined
   d. Undefined

5. A _____ is a set of numbers that designate location in a given reference system, such as x,y in a planar _____ system or an x,y,z in a three-dimensional _____ system.
   a. Thing
   b. Coordinate0
   c. Undefined
   d. Undefined

6. In mathematics, the _____ (also nullspace) of an operator A is the set of all operands v which solve the equation Av = 0. It is also called the kernel of A.

a. Thing
b. Null space0
c. Undefined
d. Undefined

7. In mathematics, the _____ of a function is the set of all "output" values produced by that function. Given a function $f : A \to B$, the _____ of f, is defined to be the set $\{x \in B : x = f(a) \text{ for some } a \in A\}$.
a. Thing
b. Range0
c. Undefined
d. Undefined

8. _____ is a set, with some particular properties and usually some additional structure, such as the operations of addition or multiplication, for instance.
a. Space0
b. Thing
c. Undefined
d. Undefined

9. In mathematics, a _____ is a constant multiplicative factor of a certain object. The object can be such things as a variable, a vector, a function, etc. For example, the _____ of $9x^2$ is 9.
a. Thing
b. Coefficient0
c. Undefined
d. Undefined

10. The word _____ comes from the Latin word linearis, which means created by lines.
a. Linear0
b. Thing
c. Undefined
d. Undefined

11. In mathematics, a linear map also called a _____ or linear operator is a function between two vector spaces that preserves the operations of vector addition and scalar multiplication.

Chapter 2. Linear Transformations and Matrices

a. Linear transformation0
b. Thing
c. Undefined
d. Undefined

12. In mathematics, a _____ is a rectangular table of numbers or, more generally, a table consisting of abstract quantities that can be added and multiplied.
a. Matrix0
b. Thing
c. Undefined
d. Undefined

13. In mathematics and the mathematical sciences, a _____ is a fixed, but possibly unspecified, value. This is in contrast to a variable, which is not fixed.
a. Thing
b. Constant0
c. Undefined
d. Undefined

14. A _____ is traditionally an infinitesimally small change in a variable.
a. Thing
b. Differential0
c. Undefined
d. Undefined

15. A _____ is a mathematical equation for an unknown function of one or several variables which relates the values of the function itself and of its derivatives of various orders.
a. Thing
b. Differential equation0
c. Undefined
d. Undefined

16. In mathematics, the _____ of a function f : X →' Y is the set Y.

Chapter 2. Linear Transformations and Matrices

a. Codomain0
b. Thing
c. Undefined
d. Undefined

17. The mathematical concept of a _____ expresses the intuitive idea of deterministic dependence between two quantities, one of which is viewed as primary and the other as secondary. A _____ then is a way to associate a unique output for each input of a specified type, for example, a real number or an element of a given set.
    a. Function0
    b. Thing
    c. Undefined
    d. Undefined

18. In mathematics, a _____ of a k-place relation $L \subseteq X_1 \times ... \times X_k$ is one of the sets X_j, $1 \leq j \leq k$. In the special case where k = 2 and $L \subseteq X_1 \times X_2$ is a function $L : X_1 \rightarrow X_2$, it is conventional to refer to X_1 as the _____ of the function and to refer to X_2 as the codomain of the function.
    a. Domain0
    b. Thing
    c. Undefined
    d. Undefined

19. In mathematics, a _____ number is a number which can be expressed as a ratio of two integers. Non-integer _____ numbers (commonly called fractions) are usually written as the vulgar fraction a / b, where b is not zero.
    a. Rational0
    b. Thing
    c. Undefined
    d. Undefined

20. In mathematics, a _____ is any one of several different types of functions, mappings, operations, or transformations.
    a. Projection0
    b. Thing
    c. Undefined
    d. Undefined

21. In mathematics, a _____ (also spelled reflexion) is a map that transforms an object into its mirror image.

Chapter 2. Linear Transformations and Matrices

a. Reflection0
b. Concept
c. Undefined
d. Undefined

22. _____ is a branch of mathematics concerning the study of structure, relation and quantity.
a. Algebra0
b. Concept
c. Undefined
d. Undefined

23. In mathematics, the _____(e) for L-functions are a class of summation formulae, expressing sums taken over the complex number zeroes of a given L-function, typically in terms of quantities studied by number theory by use of the theory of special functions.
a. Thing
b. Explicit formula0
c. Undefined
d. Undefined

24. A _____ is a movement of an object in a circular motion. A two-dimensional object rotates around a center (or point) of _____. A three-dimensional object rotates around a line called an axis. If the axis of _____ is within the body, the body is said to rotate upon itself, or spin—which implies relative speed and perhaps free-movement with angular momentum. A circular motion about an external point, e.g. the Earth about the Sun, is called an orbit or more properly an orbital revolution.
a. Thing
b. Rotation0
c. Undefined
d. Undefined

25. In statistics, a _____ measure is one which is measuring what is supposed to measure.
a. Valid0
b. Thing
c. Undefined
d. Undefined

26. In linear algebra, the _____ of a matrix A is another matrix AT

Chapter 2. Linear Transformations and Matrices

a. Thing
b. Transpose0
c. Undefined
d. Undefined

27. The _____ is a measurement of how a function changes when the values of its inputs change.
a. Derivative0
b. Thing
c. Undefined
d. Undefined

28. A _____ function is a function for which, intuitively, small changes in the input result in small changes in the output.
a. Continuous0
b. Event
c. Undefined
d. Undefined

29. An _____ is an equality that remains true regardless of the values of any variables that appear within it, to distinguish it from an equality which is true under more particular conditions.
a. Identity0
b. Thing
c. Undefined
d. Undefined

30. In mathematics, a _____ is a statement that can be proved on the basis of explicitly stated or previously agreed assumptions.
a. Theorem0
b. Thing
c. Undefined
d. Undefined

31. Mathematical _____ is used to represent ideas.

Chapter 2. Linear Transformations and Matrices

a. Notation0
b. Thing
c. Undefined
d. Undefined

32. _____ are objects, characters, or other concrete representations of ideas, concepts, or other abstractions.
a. Symbols0
b. Thing
c. Undefined
d. Undefined

33. In linear algebra and related areas of mathematics, the null vector or _____ is the vector in Euclidean space, all of whose components are zero.
a. Zero vector0
b. Thing
c. Undefined
d. Undefined

34. In mathematics, a _____ is a demonstration that, assuming certain axioms, some statement is necessarily true.
a. Thing
b. Proof0
c. Undefined
d. Undefined

35. In mathematics, a set is called _____ if there is a bijection between the set and some set of the form {1, 2, ..., n} where n is a natural number.
a. Finite0
b. Thing
c. Undefined
d. Undefined

36. In mathematics, science including computer science, linguistics and engineering, an _____ is, generally speaking, an independent variable or input to a function.

Chapter 2. Linear Transformations and Matrices

a. Thing
b. Argument0
c. Undefined
d. Undefined

37. Two mathematical objects are equal if and only if they are precisely the same in every way. This defines a binary relation, _____, denoted by the sign of _____ "=" in such a way that the statement "x = y" means that x and y are equal.
a. Thing
b. Equality0
c. Undefined
d. Undefined

38. Equivalence is the condition of being _____ or essentially equal.
a. Thing
b. Equivalent0
c. Undefined
d. Undefined

39. A _____ is a set whose members are members of another set or a set contained within another set.
a. Thing
b. Subset0
c. Undefined
d. Undefined

40. In mathematics, a _____ is an expression that is constructed from one or more variables and constants, using only the operations of addition, subtraction, multiplication, and constant positive whole number exponents. is a _____. Note in particular that division by an expression containing a variable is not in general allowed in polynomials. [1]
a. Polynomial0
b. Thing
c. Undefined
d. Undefined

41. In linear algebra, real numbers are called scalars and relate to vectors in a vector space through the operation of _____ multiplication, in which a vector can be multiplied by a number to produce another vector.

Chapter 2. Linear Transformations and Matrices

a. Scalar0
b. Thing
c. Undefined
d. Undefined

42. In mathematics, a _____ is the result of multiplying, or an expression that identifies factors to be multiplied.
a. Product0
b. Thing
c. Undefined
d. Undefined

43. A _____ is the result of the addition of a set of numbers. The numbers may be natural numbers, complex numbers, matrices, or still more complicated objects. An infinite _____ is a subtle procedure known as a series.
a. Sum0
b. Thing
c. Undefined
d. Undefined

44. _____ are groups whose members are members of another set or a set contained within another set.
a. Subsets0
b. Thing
c. Undefined
d. Undefined

45. In mathematics and logic, a _____ proof is a way of showing the truth or falsehood of a given statement by a straightforward combination of established facts, usually existing lemmas and theorems, without making any further assumptions.
a. Thing
b. Direct0
c. Undefined
d. Undefined

46. In a mathematical proof or a syllogism, a _____ is a statement that is the logical consequence of preceding statements.

a. Concept
b. Conclusion0
c. Undefined
d. Undefined

47. In mathematics, the _____ inverse, or opposite, of a number n is the number that, when added to n, yields zero. The _____ inverse of n is denoted −n.
a. Additive0
b. Thing
c. Undefined
d. Undefined

48. An _____ is a function that preserves the addition operation: f(x+y) = f(x)+f(y) for any two elements x and y in the domain.
a. Thing
b. Additive function0
c. Undefined
d. Undefined

49. In mathematics, a _____ may be described informally as a number that can be given by an infinite decimal representation.
a. Real number0
b. Thing
c. Undefined
d. Undefined

50. A _____ is a mathematical statement which follows easily from a previously proven statement, typically a mathematical theorem.
a. Corollary0
b. Thing
c. Undefined
d. Undefined

51. In mathematics, a _____ is an ordered list of objects. Like a set, it contains members, also called elements or terms, and the number of terms is called the length of the _____. Unlike a set, order matters, and the exact same elements can appear multiple times at different positions in the _____.

Chapter 2. Linear Transformations and Matrices

a. Thing
b. Sequence0
c. Undefined
d. Undefined

52. In mathematics, a matrix can be thought of as each row or _____ being a vector. Hence, a space formed by row vectors or _____ vectors are said to be a row space or a _____ space.
a. Concept
b. Column0
c. Undefined
d. Undefined

53. _____ is one of the basic operations defining a vector space in linear algebra.
a. Thing
b. Scalar multiplication0
c. Undefined
d. Undefined

54. An _____ is any starting assumption from which other statements are logically derived
a. Axiom0
b. Thing
c. Undefined
d. Undefined

55. _____, a field in mathematics, is the study of how functions change when their inputs change. The primary object of study in _____ is the derivative.
a. Thing
b. Differential calculus0
c. Undefined
d. Undefined

56. In mathematics, a _____ is a number in the form of a + bi where a and b are real numbers, and i is the imaginary unit, with the property i 2 = −1. The real number a is called the real part of the _____, and the real number b is the imaginary part.

Chapter 2. Linear Transformations and Matrices

a. Complex number0
b. Thing
c. Undefined
d. Undefined

57. In algebra, a _____ is a binomial formed by taking the opposite of the second term of a binomial.
a. Thing
b. Conjugate0
c. Undefined
d. Undefined

58. In mathematics, particularly linear algebra, a _____ is a matrix with all its entries being zero.
a. Zero matrix0
b. Thing
c. Undefined
d. Undefined

59. A _____ can refer to a line joining two nonadjacent vertices of a polygon or polyhedron, or in some contexts any upward or downward sloping line. .
a. Diagonal0
b. Thing
c. Undefined
d. Undefined

60. _____ is a square matrix in which the entries outside the main diagonal are all zero.
a. Diagonal matrix0
b. Thing
c. Undefined
d. Undefined

61. A _____ of a number is the product of that number with any integer.

a. Thing
b. Multiple0
c. Undefined
d. Undefined

62. In mathematics, a _____ of a positive integer n is a way of writing n as a sum of positive integers.
a. Composition0
b. Thing
c. Undefined
d. Undefined

63. A _____ number is a positive integer which has a positive divisor other than one or itself.
a. Composite0
b. Thing
c. Undefined
d. Undefined

64. In mathematics, an identity function, also called identity map or _____, is a function that does not have any effect: it always returns the same value that was used as its argument. In other words, the identity function is the function f = x.
a. Thing
b. Identity transformation0
c. Undefined
d. Undefined

65. _____ is a mathematical subject that includes the study of limits, derivatives, integrals, and power series and constitutes a major part of modern university curriculum.
a. Calculus0
b. Thing
c. Undefined
d. Undefined

66. In mathematics, the _____ inverse of a number x, denoted 1/x or x^{-1}, is the number which, when multiplied by x, yields 1. The _____ inverse of x is also called the reciprocal of x.

Chapter 2. Linear Transformations and Matrices

   a. Thing
   b. Multiplicative0
   c. Undefined
   d. Undefined

67. A _____ is a number, figure, or indicator that appears below the normal line of type, typically used in a formula, mathematical expression, or description of a chemical compound.
   a. Subscript0
   b. Thing
   c. Undefined
   d. Undefined

68. In mathematics, the notion of _____ is a generalization of the notion of invertible.
   a. Thing
   b. Cancellation0
   c. Undefined
   d. Undefined

69. _____ is an m × 1 matrix, i.e. a matrix consisting of a single column of m elements.
   a. Thing
   b. Column vector0
   c. Undefined
   d. Undefined

70. _____ Logic is a concept in traditional logic referring to a "type of immediate inference in which from a given proposition another proposition is inferred which has as its subject the predicate of the original proposition and as its predicate the subject of the original proposition (the quality of the proposition being retained)."
   a. Concept
   b. Converse0
   c. Undefined
   d. Undefined

71. In mathematics, _____ is a property that a binary operation can have. Within an expression containing two or more of the same associative operators in a row, the order of operations does not matter as long as the sequence of the operands is not changed.

Chapter 2. Linear Transformations and Matrices

a. Associativity0
b. Thing
c. Undefined
d. Undefined

72. In geometry, the relations of _____ are those such as 'lies on' between points and lines (as in 'point P lies on line L'), and 'intersects' (as in 'line L_1 intersects line L_2', in three-dimensional space). That is, they are the binary relations describing how subsets meet.
a. Incidence0
b. Thing
c. Undefined
d. Undefined

73. In plane geometry, a _____ is a polygon with four equal sides, four right angles, and parallel opposite sides. In algebra, the _____ of a number is that number multiplied by itself.
a. Square0
b. Thing
c. Undefined
d. Undefined

74. _____ is an informal and restricted social group formed by people who share common interests.
a. Thing
b. Clique0
c. Undefined
d. Undefined

75. _____ the expected value of a random variable displays the average or central value of the variable. It is a summary value of the distribution of the variable.
a. Determining0
b. Thing
c. Undefined
d. Undefined

76. In mathematics, the conjugate _____ or adjoint matrix of an m-by-n matrix A with complex entries is the n-by-m matrix A* obtained from A by taking the transpose and then taking the complex conjugate of each entry.

Chapter 2. Linear Transformations and Matrices

   a. Pairs0
   b. Thing
   c. Undefined
   d. Undefined

77. _____ is the study of terms and their use — of words and compound words that are used in specific contexts.
   a. Terminology0
   b. Thing
   c. Undefined
   d. Undefined

78. In linear algebra, the _____ of an n-by-n square matrix A is defined to be the sum of the elements on the main diagonal of A,
   a. Trace0
   b. Thing
   c. Undefined
   d. Undefined

79. In combinatorial mathematics, a _____ is an un-ordered collection of unique elements.
   a. Concept
   b. Combination0
   c. Undefined
   d. Undefined

80. _____ element of an element x with respect to a binary operation * with identity element e is an element y such that x * y = y * x = e. In particular,
   a. Inverse0
   b. Thing
   c. Undefined
   d. Undefined

81. In mathematics, the idea of _____ generalises the concepts of negation, in relation to addition, and reciprocal, in relation to multiplication.

Chapter 2. Linear Transformations and Matrices

a. Inverse element0
b. Thing
c. Undefined
d. Undefined

82. In mathematics, an _____ (Greek:isos "equal", and morphe "shape") is a bijective map f such that both f and its inverse f $^{-1}$ are homomorphisms, i.e. *structure-preserving* mappings.
a. Isomorphism0
b. Thing
c. Undefined
d. Undefined

83. _____ is a method of constructing new data points from a discrete set of known data points.
a. Thing
b. Interpolation0
c. Undefined
d. Undefined

84. _____ is the state of being greater than any finite real or natural number, however large.
a. Thing
b. Infinite0
c. Undefined
d. Undefined

85. Mathematical _____ are the wide variety of ways to capture an abstract mathematical concept or relationship.
a. Thing
b. Representations0
c. Undefined
d. Undefined

86. A _____ is a simplified and structured visual representation of concepts, ideas, constructions, relations, statistical data, anatomy etc used in all aspects of human activities to visualize and clarify the topic.

Chapter 2. Linear Transformations and Matrices

   a. Diagram0
   b. Thing
   c. Undefined
   d. Undefined

87. The _____, the average in everyday English, which is also called the arithmetic _____ (and is distinguished from the geometric _____ or harmonic _____). The average is also called the sample _____. The expected value of a random variable, which is also called the population _____.
   a. Thing
   b. Mean0
   c. Undefined
   d. Undefined

88. An _____ is a binary relation between two elements of a set which groups them together as being equivalent in some way.
   a. Equivalence relation0
   b. Thing
   c. Undefined
   d. Undefined

89. In numerical analysis, a _____, named after Joseph Louis Lagrange, is the interpolation polynomial for a given set of data points in the Lagrange form.
   a. Lagrange polynomial0
   b. Thing
   c. Undefined
   d. Undefined

90. A _____ is a symbolic representation denoting a quantity or expression. It often represents an "unknown" quantity that has the potential to change.
   a. Thing
   b. Variable0
   c. Undefined
   d. Undefined

91. An _____ is a combination of numbers, operators, grouping symbols and/or free variables and bound variables arranged in a meaningful way which can be evaluated..

a. Expression0
b. Thing
c. Undefined
d. Undefined

92. In mathematics, a _____ is a two-dimensional manifold or surface that is perfectly flat.
a. Plane0
b. Thing
c. Undefined
d. Undefined

93. _____ in a normed vector space is a vector whose length, or magnitude is 1.
a. Unit vector0
b. Thing
c. Undefined
d. Undefined

94. An _____ is a square matrix which has an inverse.
a. Invertible matrix0
b. Thing
c. Undefined
d. Undefined

95. In elementary algebra, an _____ is a set that contains every real number between two indicated numbers and may contain the two numbers themselves.
a. Interval0
b. Thing
c. Undefined
d. Undefined

96. In mathematics, the term _____ is applied to certain functions. There are two common ways it is applied: these are related historically, but diverged somewhat during the twentieth century.

a. Functional0
b. Thing
c. Undefined
d. Undefined

97. In mathematics, the _____ of a coordinate system is the point where the axes of the system intersect.
a. Origin0
b. Thing
c. Undefined
d. Undefined

98. A _____ fraction is a fraction in which the absolute value of the numerator is less than the denominator--hence, the absolute value of the fraction is less than 1.
a. Thing
b. Proper0
c. Undefined
d. Undefined

99. In economics, economic _____ is simply a state of the world where economic forces are balanced and in the absence of external influences the values of economic variables will not change.
a. Equilibrium0
b. Thing
c. Undefined
d. Undefined

100. In physics, _____ is an influence that may cause an object to accelerate. It may be experienced as a lift, a push, or a pull. The actual acceleration of the body is determined by the vector sum of all forces acting on it, known as net _____ or resultant _____.
a. Force0
b. Thing
c. Undefined
d. Undefined

101. In mathematics, the _____ of a complex number z, is the first element of the ordered pair of real numbers representing z, i.e. if z = (x,y), or equivalently, z = x + iy, then the _____ of z is x. It is denoted by Re{z} . The complex function which maps z to the _____ of z is not holomorphic.

a. Real part0
b. Thing
c. Undefined
d. Undefined

102. In mathematics, an _____ number is a complex number whose square is a negative real number. They were defined in 1572 by Rafael Bombelli.
a. Thing
b. Imaginary0
c. Undefined
d. Undefined

103. In mathematics, the _____ of a complex number z, is the second element of the ordered pair of real numbers representing z, i.e. if z = (x,y), or equivalently, z = x + iy, then the _____ of z is y.
a. Thing
b. Imaginary part0
c. Undefined
d. Undefined

104. _____ is the fee paid on borrowed money.
a. Thing
b. Interest0
c. Undefined
d. Undefined

105. In mathematics, there are several meanings of _____ depending on the subject.
a. Thing
b. Degree0
c. Undefined
d. Undefined

106. In mathematics, _____ growth occurs when the growth rate of a function is always proportional to the function's current size.

a. Exponential0
b. Thing
c. Undefined
d. Undefined

107. _____ is one of the most important functions in mathematics. A function commonly used to study growth and decay
a. Exponential function0
b. Thing
c. Undefined
d. Undefined

108. _____ is a function whose values do not vary and thus are constant.
a. Thing
b. Constant function0
c. Undefined
d. Undefined

109. In mathematics, factorization (British English: factorisation) or factoring is the decomposition of an object (for example, a number, a polynomial, or a matrix) into a product of other objects, or _____, which when multiplied together give the original.
a. Thing
b. Factors0
c. Undefined
d. Undefined

110. In logic, and especially in its applications to mathematics and philosophy, a _____ is an exception to a proposed general rule, i.e., a specific instance of the falsity of a universal quantification (a "for all" statement).
a. Counterexample0
b. Thing
c. Undefined
d. Undefined

111. A _____ is an equation in which each term is either a constant or the product of a constant times the first power of a variable.

Chapter 2. Linear Transformations and Matrices

a. Linear equation0
b. Thing
c. Undefined
d. Undefined

112. _____ is a method of mathematical proof typically used to establish that a given statement is true of all natural numbers
   a. Mathematical induction0
   b. Thing
   c. Undefined
   d. Undefined

113. A _____ consists either of a suggested explanation for a phenomenon or of a reasoned proposal suggesting a possible correlation between multiple phenomena.
   a. Thing
   b. Hypothesis0
   c. Undefined
   d. Undefined

114. The _____ is a unit of plane angle. It is represented by the symbol "rad" or, more rarely, by the superscript c (for "circular measure"). For example, an angle of 1.2 radians would be written "1.2 rad" or "1.2c" (second symbol can produce confusion with centigrads).
   a. Radian0
   b. Thing
   c. Undefined
   d. Undefined

115. A _____ is an object that is attached to a pivot point so that it can swing freely.
   a. Thing
   b. Pendulum0
   c. Undefined
   d. Undefined

116. The _____ of a mathematical object is its size: a property by which it can be larger or smaller than other objects of the same kind; in technical terms, an ordering of the class of objects to which it belongs.

Chapter 2. Linear Transformations and Matrices

a. Magnitude0
b. Thing
c. Undefined
d. Undefined

117. _____ is defined as the rate of change or derivative with respect to time of velocity.
a. Thing
b. Acceleration0
c. Undefined
d. Undefined

118. The _____ of measurement are a globally standardized and modernized form of the metric system.
a. Thing
b. Units0
c. Undefined
d. Undefined

119. The metre (or _____, see spelling differences) is a measure of length. It is the basic unit of length in the metric system and in the International System of Units (SI), used around the world for general and scientific purposes.
a. Meter0
b. Concept
c. Undefined
d. Undefined

120. In mathematics, two quantities are called _____ if they vary in such a way that one of the quantities is a constant multiple of the other, or equivalently if they have a constant ratio.
a. Proportional0
b. Thing
c. Undefined
d. Undefined

121. In mathematics, the additive inverse, or _____ of a number n is the number that, when added to n, yields zero. The additive inverse of n is denoted −n. For example, 7 is −7, because 7 + (−7) = 0, and the additive inverse of −0.3 is 0.3, because −0.3 + 0.3 = 0.

Chapter 2. Linear Transformations and Matrices

a. Thing
b. Opposite0
c. Undefined
d. Undefined

122. In mathematics, the _____ of a number n is the number that, when added to n, yields zero. The _____ of n is denoted −n. For example, 7 is −7, because 7 + (−7) = 0, and the _____ of −0.3 is 0.3, because −0.3 + 0.3 = 0.
a. Thing
b. Additive inverse0
c. Undefined
d. Undefined

123. _____ of an object is its speed in a particular direction.
a. Thing
b. Velocity0
c. Undefined
d. Undefined

124. Initial objects are also called _____, and terminal objects are also called final.
a. Coterminal0
b. Thing
c. Undefined
d. Undefined

125. The word _____ is used in a variety of ways in mathematics.
a. Index0
b. Thing
c. Undefined
d. Undefined

126. In mathematics, in the field of differential equations, an initial value problem is a differential equation together with specified value, called the _____, of the unknown function at a given point in the domain of the solution.

Chapter 2. Linear Transformations and Matrices

a. Initial condition0
b. Thing
c. Undefined
d. Undefined

127. The _____ is a nonnegative scalar measure of a wave's magnitude of oscillation, that is, the magnitude of the maximum disturbance in the medium during one wave cycle.
a. Amplitude0
b. Thing
c. Undefined
d. Undefined

128. The _____ governs the differentiation of products of differentiable functions.
a. Product rule0
b. Thing
c. Undefined
d. Undefined

Chapter 3. Elementary Matrix Operations and Systems of Linear Equations

1. In mathematics, a _____ in elementary terms is any of a variety of different functions from geometry, such as rotations, reflections and translations.
   a. Thing
   b. Transformation0
   c. Undefined
   d. Undefined

2. In physics and in _____ calculus, a spatial _____, or simply _____, is a concept characterized by a magnitude and a direction.
   a. Vector0
   b. Thing
   c. Undefined
   d. Undefined

3. _____ is a collection of objects called vectors that, informally speaking, may be scaled and added.
   a. Thing
   b. Vector space0
   c. Undefined
   d. Undefined

4. _____ is a set, with some particular properties and usually some additional structure, such as the operations of addition or multiplication, for instance.
   a. Space0
   b. Thing
   c. Undefined
   d. Undefined

5. The word _____ comes from the Latin word linearis, which means created by lines.
   a. Thing
   b. Linear0
   c. Undefined
   d. Undefined

6. In mathematics, a linear map also called a _____ or linear operator is a function between two vector spaces that preserves the operations of vector addition and scalar multiplication.

Chapter 3. Elementary Matrix Operations and Systems of Linear Equations

  a. Thing
  b. Linear transformation0
  c. Undefined
  d. Undefined

7. In mathematics, a _____ is a rectangular table of numbers or, more generally, a table consisting of abstract quantities that can be added and multiplied.
  a. Matrix0
  b. Thing
  c. Undefined
  d. Undefined

8. In mathematics, a set is called _____ if there is a bijection between the set and some set of the form {1, 2, ..., n} where n is a natural number.
  a. Thing
  b. Finite0
  c. Undefined
  d. Undefined

9. A _____ is an equation in which each term is either a constant or the product of a constant times the first power of a variable.
  a. Linear equation0
  b. Thing
  c. Undefined
  d. Undefined

10. _____ is a branch of mathematics concerning the study of structure, relation and quantity.
  a. Algebra0
  b. Concept
  c. Undefined
  d. Undefined

11. A _____ of a number is the product of that number with any integer.

Chapter 3. Elementary Matrix Operations and Systems of Linear Equations

   a. Multiple0
   b. Thing
   c. Undefined
   d. Undefined

12. A _____ is a symbolic representation denoting a quantity or expression. It often represents an "unknown" quantity that has the potential to change.
   a. Variable0
   b. Thing
   c. Undefined
   d. Undefined

13. In mathematics and the mathematical sciences, a _____ is a fixed, but possibly unspecified, value. This is in contrast to a variable, which is not fixed.
   a. Thing
   b. Constant0
   c. Undefined
   d. Undefined

14. _____ the expected value of a random variable displays the average or central value of the variable. It is a summary value of the distribution of the variable.
   a. Determining0
   b. Thing
   c. Undefined
   d. Undefined

15. In mathematics, a matrix can be thought of as each row or _____ being a vector. Hence, a space formed by row vectors or _____ vectors are said to be a row space or a _____ space.
   a. Column0
   b. Concept
   c. Undefined
   d. Undefined

16. Elementary _____ are simple transformations which can be applied to a matrix without changing the linear system of equations that it represents.

a. Row operations0
b. Thing
c. Undefined
d. Undefined

17. The _____, the average in everyday English, which is also called the arithmetic _____ (and is distinguished from the geometric _____ or harmonic _____). The average is also called the sample _____. The expected value of a random variable, which is also called the population _____.
   a. Mean0
   b. Thing
   c. Undefined
   d. Undefined

18. Equivalence is the condition of being _____ or essentially equal.
   a. Equivalent0
   b. Thing
   c. Undefined
   d. Undefined

19. In mathematics, a _____ is a statement that can be proved on the basis of explicitly stated or previously agreed assumptions.
   a. Theorem0
   b. Thing
   c. Undefined
   d. Undefined

20. In mathematics, a _____ is a demonstration that, assuming certain axioms, some statement is necessarily true.
   a. Proof0
   b. Thing
   c. Undefined
   d. Undefined

21. In linear algebra, the _____ of a matrix A is another matrix AT

a. Transpose0
b. Thing
c. Undefined
d. Undefined

22. _____ element of an element x with respect to a binary operation * with identity element e is an element y such that x * y = y * x = e. In particular,
a. Thing
b. Inverse0
c. Undefined
d. Undefined

23. In mathematics, the idea of _____ generalises the concepts of negation, in relation to addition, and reciprocal, in relation to multiplication.
a. Inverse element0
b. Thing
c. Undefined
d. Undefined

24. In plane geometry, a _____ is a polygon with four equal sides, four right angles, and parallel opposite sides. In algebra, the _____ of a number is that number multiplied by itself.
a. Square0
b. Thing
c. Undefined
d. Undefined

25. An _____ is an equality that remains true regardless of the values of any variables that appear within it, to distinguish it from an equality which is true under more particular conditions.
a. Thing
b. Identity0
c. Undefined
d. Undefined

26. In mathematics, a _____ is the result of multiplying, or an expression that identifies factors to be multiplied.

56 Chapter 3. Elementary Matrix Operations and Systems of Linear Equations

   a. Product0
   b. Thing
   c. Undefined
   d. Undefined

27. A _____ is the result of the addition of a set of numbers. The numbers may be natural numbers, complex numbers, matrices, or still more complicated objects. An infinite _____ is a subtle procedure known as a series.
   a. Thing
   b. Sum0
   c. Undefined
   d. Undefined

28. In linear algebra, real numbers are called scalars and relate to vectors in a vector space through the operation of _____ multiplication, in which a vector can be multiplied by a number to produce another vector.
   a. Thing
   b. Scalar0
   c. Undefined
   d. Undefined

29. _____ is a special kind of square matrix where the entries below or above the main diagonal are zero.
   a. Triangular form0
   b. Thing
   c. Undefined
   d. Undefined

30. In mathematics, a _____ is an ordered list of objects. Like a set, it contains members, also called elements or terms, and the number of terms is called the length of the _____. Unlike a set, order matters, and the exact same elements can appear multiple times at different positions in the _____.
   a. Thing
   b. Sequence0
   c. Undefined
   d. Undefined

31. _____ are elementary linear transformations on a matrix which preserve matrix equivalence.

Chapter 3. Elementary Matrix Operations and Systems of Linear Equations

a. Thing
b. Elementary row operations0
c. Undefined
d. Undefined

32. A _____ is a mathematical statement which follows easily from a previously proven statement, typically a mathematical theorem.
a. Thing
b. Corollary0
c. Undefined
d. Undefined

33. In combinatorial mathematics, a _____ is an un-ordered collection of unique elements.
a. Concept
b. Combination0
c. Undefined
d. Undefined

34. _____ has many meanings, most of which simply .
a. Power0
b. Thing
c. Undefined
d. Undefined

35. A _____ consists either of a suggested explanation for a phenomenon or of a reasoned proposal suggesting a possible correlation between multiple phenomena.
a. Hypothesis0
b. Thing
c. Undefined
d. Undefined

36. A _____ can refer to a line joining two nonadjacent vertices of a polygon or polyhedron, or in some contexts any upward or downward sloping line. .

Chapter 3. Elementary Matrix Operations and Systems of Linear Equations

a. Thing
b. Diagonal0
c. Undefined
d. Undefined

37. An _____ is a square matrix which has an inverse.
   a. Thing
   b. Invertible matrix0
   c. Undefined
   d. Undefined

38. Acid _____ ratio measures the ability of a company to use its near cash or quick assets to immediately extinguish its current liabilities.
   a. Test0
   b. Thing
   c. Undefined
   d. Undefined

39. The _____ is a measurement of how a function changes when the values of its inputs change.
   a. Thing
   b. Derivative0
   c. Undefined
   d. Undefined

40. In mathematics, particularly linear algebra, a _____ is a matrix with all its entries being zero.
   a. Thing
   b. Zero matrix0
   c. Undefined
   d. Undefined

41. A _____ is a set whose members are members of another set or a set contained within another set.

Chapter 3. Elementary Matrix Operations and Systems of Linear Equations

 a. Thing
 b. Subset0
 c. Undefined
 d. Undefined

42. _____ are groups whose members are members of another set or a set contained within another set.
 a. Subsets0
 b. Thing
 c. Undefined
 d. Undefined

43. In mathematics, the word _____ is used informally to refer to certain distinct bodies of knowledge about mathematics.
 a. Theoretical0
 b. Thing
 c. Undefined
 d. Undefined

44. The easiest _____ prime numbers resides in the use of the Sieve of Eratosthenes, an algorithm that discovers all prime numbers to a specified integer.
 a. Method for finding0
 b. Thing
 c. Undefined
 d. Undefined

45. In mathematics, a _____ is a constant multiplicative factor of a certain object. The object can be such things as a variable, a vector, a function, etc. For example, the _____ of $9x^2$ is 9.
 a. Coefficient0
 b. Thing
 c. Undefined
 d. Undefined

46. In linear algebra, the _____ refers to a matrix consisting of the coefficients of the variables in a set of linear equations.

Chapter 3. Elementary Matrix Operations and Systems of Linear Equations

a. Coefficient matrix0
b. Thing
c. Undefined
d. Undefined

47. A _____ is a set of possible values that a variable can take on in order to satisfy a given set of conditions, which may include equations and inequalities.
a. Solution set0
b. Thing
c. Undefined
d. Undefined

48. In linear algebra and related areas of mathematics, the null vector or _____ is the vector in Euclidean space, all of whose components are zero.
a. Thing
b. Zero vector0
c. Undefined
d. Undefined

49. There are two simple _____ the greatest common factor and least common multiple: standard factorization and prime factorization.
a. Thing
b. Methods for finding0
c. Undefined
d. Undefined

50. In common philosophical language, a proposition or _____, is the content of an assertion, that is, it is true-or-false and defined by the meaning of a particular piece of language.
a. Statement0
b. Concept
c. Undefined
d. Undefined

51. In mathematics, the _____ of a function is the set of all "output" values produced by that function. Given a function $f : A \to B$, the _____ of f, is defined to be the set $\{x \in B : x = f(a)$ for some $a \in A\}$.

Chapter 3. Elementary Matrix Operations and Systems of Linear Equations

a. Thing
b. Range0
c. Undefined
d. Undefined

52. In linear algebra, the _____ of a matrix is obtained by combining two matrices in such a way that a matrix of coefficients to which has been added a column of constants corresponds to the right hand side of the equations.
   a. Augmented matrix0
   b. Thing
   c. Undefined
   d. Undefined

53. _____ was an economist notable for his research on how changes in one economic sector may have an effect on other sectors. Leontief won a Nobel Prize in Economics in 1973.
   a. Person
   b. Wassily Leontief0
   c. Undefined
   d. Undefined

54. A _____ is an abstract model that uses mathematical language to describe the behavior of a system. Eykhoff defined a _____ as 'a representation of the essential aspects of an existing system which presents knowledge of that system in usable form'.
   a. Thing
   b. Mathematical model0
   c. Undefined
   d. Undefined

55. The _____ integers are all the integers from zero on upwards.
   a. Nonnegative0
   b. Thing
   c. Undefined
   d. Undefined

56. In economics, economic _____ is simply a state of the world where economic forces are balanced and in the absence of external influences the values of economic variables will not change.

Chapter 3. Elementary Matrix Operations and Systems of Linear Equations

a. Thing
b. Equilibrium0
c. Undefined
d. Undefined

57. In mathematics, an _____ is a statement about the relative size or order of two objects.
    a. Inequality0
    b. Thing
    c. Undefined
    d. Undefined

58. _____ (or proportionality) are two quantities that vary in such a way that one of the quatities is a constant multiple of the other, or equivalently if they have a constant ratio.
    a. Proportions0
    b. Thing
    c. Undefined
    d. Undefined

59. _____ is a kind of property which exists as magnitude or multitude. It is among the basic classes of things along with quality, substance, change, and relation.
    a. Thing
    b. Amount0
    c. Undefined
    d. Undefined

60. In economics, supply and _____ describe market relations between prospective sellers and buyers of a good.
    a. Demand0
    b. Thing
    c. Undefined
    d. Undefined

61. A _____ is the sum of the elements of a sequence.

Chapter 3. Elementary Matrix Operations and Systems of Linear Equations

a. Series0
b. Thing
c. Undefined
d. Undefined

62. _____ denotes the approach toward a definite value, as time goes on; or to a definite point, a common view or opinion, or toward a fixed or equilibrium state.
a. Thing
b. Convergence0
c. Undefined
d. Undefined

63. In mathematics, a _____ may be described informally as a number that can be given by an infinite decimal representation.
a. Real number0
b. Thing
c. Undefined
d. Undefined

64. In economics _____ means before deductions brutto, e.g. _____ domestic or national product, or _____ profit or income
a. Thing
b. Gross0
c. Undefined
d. Undefined

65. A circular _____ or circle _____ also known as a pie piece is the portion of a circle enclosed by two radii and an arc.
a. Thing
b. Sector0
c. Undefined
d. Undefined

66. In mathematics, _____ refers to the rewriting of an expression into a simpler form.

Chapter 3. Elementary Matrix Operations and Systems of Linear Equations

a. Thing
b. Reduction0
c. Undefined
d. Undefined

67. A _____ is a matrix form used when solving linear systems of equations.
a. Thing
b. Row echelon form0
c. Undefined
d. Undefined

68. In mathematics, a matrix is in row _____ if is satisfies the following requirements: • All nonzero rows are above any rows of all zeroes. • The leading coefficient of a row is always strictly to the right of the leading coefficient of the row above it.
a. Thing
b. Echelon form0
c. Undefined
d. Undefined

69. _____ is an algorithm which can be used to determine the solutions of a system of linear equations, to find the rank of a matrix, and to calculate the inverse of an invertible square matrix.
a. Thing
b. Gaussian elimination0
c. Undefined
d. Undefined

70. _____ or arithmetics is the oldest and most elementary branch of mathematics, used by almost everyone, for tasks ranging from simple daily counting to advanced science and business calculations.
a. Thing
b. Arithmetic0
c. Undefined
d. Undefined

71. The traditional _____ are addition, subtraction, multiplication and division, although more advanced operations (such as manipulations of percentages, square root, exponentiation, and logarithmic functions) are also sometimes included in this subject.

a. Concept
b. Arithmetic operations0
c. Undefined
d. Undefined

72. _____ is the study of algorithms for the problems of continuous mathematics as distinguished from discrete mathematics.
   a. Numerical analysis0
   b. Thing
   c. Undefined
   d. Undefined

73. A _____ is the quantity that defines certain relatively constant characteristics of systems or functions..
   a. Parameter0
   b. Thing
   c. Undefined
   d. Undefined

74. A _____ is a set of numbers that designate location in a given reference system, such as x,y in a planar _____ system or an x,y,z in a three-dimensional _____ system.
   a. Coordinate0
   b. Thing
   c. Undefined
   d. Undefined

Chapter 4. Determinants of Order

1. _____ is an adjective usually refering to being in the centre.
   a. Thing
   b. Central0
   c. Undefined
   d. Undefined

2. The word _____ comes from the Latin word linearis, which means created by lines.
   a. Linear0
   b. Thing
   c. Undefined
   d. Undefined

3. _____ is a branch of mathematics concerning the study of structure, relation and quantity.
   a. Algebra0
   b. Concept
   c. Undefined
   d. Undefined

4. In mathematics, an _____ on a real vector space is a choice of which ordered bases are "positively" oriented, or right-handed, and which are "negatively" oriented, or left-handed.
   a. Thing
   b. Orientation0
   c. Undefined
   d. Undefined

5. In algebra, a _____ is a function depending on n that associates a scalar, $\det(A)$, to every $n \times n$ square matrix A.
   a. Thing
   b. Determinant0
   c. Undefined
   d. Undefined

6. In plane geometry, a _____ is a polygon with four equal sides, four right angles, and parallel opposite sides. In algebra, the _____ of a number is that number multiplied by itself.

a. Thing
b. Square0
c. Undefined
d. Undefined

7. In mathematics, a _____ is a rectangular table of numbers or, more generally, a table consisting of abstract quantities that can be added and multiplied.
a. Matrix0
b. Thing
c. Undefined
d. Undefined

8. In linear algebra, real numbers are called scalars and relate to vectors in a vector space through the operation of _____ multiplication, in which a vector can be multiplied by a number to produce another vector.
a. Scalar0
b. Thing
c. Undefined
d. Undefined

9. In mathematics, a _____ in elementary terms is any of a variety of different functions from geometry, such as rotations, reflections and translations.
a. Transformation0
b. Thing
c. Undefined
d. Undefined

10. In mathematics, a linear map also called a _____ or linear operator is a function between two vector spaces that preserves the operations of vector addition and scalar multiplication.
a. Linear transformation0
b. Thing
c. Undefined
d. Undefined

11. The mathematical concept of a _____ expresses the intuitive idea of deterministic dependence between two quantities, one of which is viewed as primary and the other as secondary. A _____ then is a way to associate a unique output for each input of a specified type, for example, a real number or an element of a given set.

Chapter 4. Determinants of Order

   a. Function0
   b. Thing
   c. Undefined
   d. Undefined

12. A _____ is a first degree polynomial mathematical function of the form: f(x) = mx + b where m and b are real constants and x is a real variable.
   a. Thing
   b. Linear function0
   c. Undefined
   d. Undefined

13. In mathematics, a _____ is a statement that can be proved on the basis of explicitly stated or previously agreed assumptions.
   a. Thing
   b. Theorem0
   c. Undefined
   d. Undefined

14. A _____ is a deliberate process for transforming one or more inputs into one or more results.
   a. Thing
   b. Calculation0
   c. Undefined
   d. Undefined

15. In mathematics, the idea of _____ generalises the concepts of negation, in relation to addition, and reciprocal, in relation to multiplication.
   a. Inverse element0
   b. Thing
   c. Undefined
   d. Undefined

16. In mathematics, science including computer science, linguistics and engineering, an _____ is, generally speaking, an independent variable or input to a function.

Chapter 4. Determinants of Order

a. Argument0
b. Thing
c. Undefined
d. Undefined

17. In physics and in _____ calculus, a spatial _____, or simply _____, is a concept characterized by a magnitude and a direction.
   a. Vector0
   b. Thing
   c. Undefined
   d. Undefined

18. In mathematics, the _____ of a coordinate system is the point where the axes of the system intersect.
   a. Thing
   b. Origin0
   c. Undefined
   d. Undefined

19. A _____ is a four-sided plane figure that has two sets of opposite parallel sides.
   a. Concept
   b. Parallelogram0
   c. Undefined
   d. Undefined

20. The _____ of a mathematical object is its size: a property by which it can be larger or smaller than other objects of the same kind; in technical terms, an ordering of the class of objects to which it belongs.
   a. Magnitude0
   b. Thing
   c. Undefined
   d. Undefined

21. The _____, the average in everyday English, which is also called the arithmetic _____ (and is distinguished from the geometric _____ or harmonic _____). The average is also called the sample _____. The expected value of a random variable, which is also called the population _____.

Chapter 4. Determinants of Order

a. Mean0
b. Thing
c. Undefined
d. Undefined

22. A _____ is a function that assigns a number to subsets of a given set.
   a. Thing
   b. Measure0
   c. Undefined
   d. Undefined

23. In mathematics, a _____ may be described informally as a number that can be given by an infinite decimal representation.
   a. Real number0
   b. Thing
   c. Undefined
   d. Undefined

24. A _____ is the part of a fraction that tells how many equal parts make up a whole, and which is used in the name of the fraction: "halves", "thirds", "fourths" or "quarters", "fifths" and so on.
   a. Denominator0
   b. Concept
   c. Undefined
   d. Undefined

25. A _____ is a set of numbers that designate location in a given reference system, such as x,y in a planar _____ system or an x,y,z in a three-dimensional _____ system.
   a. Coordinate0
   b. Thing
   c. Undefined
   d. Undefined

26. In mathematics and its applications, a _____ is a system for assigning an n-tuple of numbers or scalars to each point in an n-dimensional space.

a. Concept
b. Coordinate system0
c. Undefined
d. Undefined

27. In logic, Modus tollens (or Modus ponendo tollens) means to affirm by denying. It is the formal name for _____ proof or proof by contrapositive (contrapositive inference), often abbreviated to MT.
   a. Indirect0
   b. Thing
   c. Undefined
   d. Undefined

28. In statistics, a _____ measure is one which is measuring what is supposed to measure.
   a. Thing
   b. Valid0
   c. Undefined
   d. Undefined

29. In geometry, an _____ of a triangle is a straight line through a vertex and perpendicular to (i.e. forming a right angle with) the opposite side or an extension of the opposite side.
   a. Altitude0
   b. Concept
   c. Undefined
   d. Undefined

30. In a mathematical proof or a syllogism, a _____ is a statement that is the logical consequence of preceding statements.
   a. Concept
   b. Conclusion0
   c. Undefined
   d. Undefined

31. In geometry, _____ angles are angles that have a common ray coming out of the vertex going between two other rays.

Chapter 4. Determinants of Order

a. Concept
b. Adjacent0
c. Undefined
d. Undefined

32. An _____ is an equality that remains true regardless of the values of any variables that appear within it, to distinguish it from an equality which is true under more particular conditions.
   a. Identity0
   b. Thing
   c. Undefined
   d. Undefined

33. In linear algebra, a _____ or minor of a matrix A is the determinant of some smaller square matrix, cut down from A.
   a. Thing
   b. Cofactor0
   c. Undefined
   d. Undefined

34. In mathematics, a matrix can be thought of as each row or _____ being a vector. Hence, a space formed by row vectors or _____ vectors are said to be a row space or a _____ space.
   a. Column0
   b. Concept
   c. Undefined
   d. Undefined

35. In mathematics, a _____ is the result of multiplying, or an expression that identifies factors to be multiplied.
   a. Product0
   b. Thing
   c. Undefined
   d. Undefined

36. _____ is a method of mathematical proof typically used to establish that a given statement is true of all natural numbers

Chapter 4. Determinants of Order

a. Thing
b. Mathematical induction0
c. Undefined
d. Undefined

37. An _____ of a product of sums expresses it as a sum of products by using the fact that multiplication distributes over addition.
a. Expansion0
b. Thing
c. Undefined
d. Undefined

38. A _____ consists either of a suggested explanation for a phenomenon or of a reasoned proposal suggesting a possible correlation between multiple phenomena.
a. Thing
b. Hypothesis0
c. Undefined
d. Undefined

39. In mathematics, a _____ is a demonstration that, assuming certain axioms, some statement is necessarily true.
a. Thing
b. Proof0
c. Undefined
d. Undefined

40. _____ are elementary linear transformations on a matrix which preserve matrix equivalence.
a. Elementary row operations0
b. Thing
c. Undefined
d. Undefined

41. Elementary _____ are simple transformations which can be applied to a matrix without changing the linear system of equations that it represents.

Chapter 4. Determinants of Order

a. Row operations0
b. Thing
c. Undefined
d. Undefined

42. A _____ is a mathematical statement which follows easily from a previously proven statement, typically a mathematical theorem.
   a. Corollary0
   b. Thing
   c. Undefined
   d. Undefined

43. A _____ of a number is the product of that number with any integer.
   a. Multiple0
   b. Thing
   c. Undefined
   d. Undefined

44. _____ Logic is a concept in traditional logic referring to a "type of immediate inference in which from a given proposition another proposition is inferred which has as its subject the predicate of the original proposition and as its predicate the subject of the original proposition (the quality of the proposition being retained)."
   a. Converse0
   b. Concept
   c. Undefined
   d. Undefined

45. _____ is a special kind of square matrix where the entries below or above the main diagonal are zero.
   a. Thing
   b. Triangular form0
   c. Undefined
   d. Undefined

46. A _____ can refer to a line joining two nonadjacent vertices of a polygon or polyhedron, or in some contexts any upward or downward sloping line. .

Chapter 4. Determinants of Order

   a. Thing
   b. Diagonal0
   c. Undefined
   d. Undefined

47. In mathematics, _____ is an elementary arithmetic operation. When one of the numbers is a whole number, _____ is the repeated sum of the other number.
   a. Multiplication0
   b. Thing
   c. Undefined
   d. Undefined

48. A _____ is the result of the addition of a set of numbers. The numbers may be natural numbers, complex numbers, matrices, or still more complicated objects. An infinite _____ is a subtle procedure known as a series.
   a. Sum0
   b. Thing
   c. Undefined
   d. Undefined

49. In mathematics, the _____ inverse of a number x, denoted 1/x or x^{-1}, is the number which, when multiplied by x, yields 1. The _____ inverse of x is also called the reciprocal of x.
   a. Thing
   b. Multiplicative0
   c. Undefined
   d. Undefined

50. Mathematical _____ is used to represent ideas.
   a. Notation0
   b. Thing
   c. Undefined
   d. Undefined

51. A _____ is an equation in which each term is either a constant or the product of a constant times the first power of a variable.

a. Linear equation0
b. Thing
c. Undefined
d. Undefined

52. The _____ are the only integral domain whose positive elements are well-ordered, and in which order is preserved by addition. Like the natural numbers, the _____ form a countably infinite set. The set of all _____ is usually denoted in mathematics by a boldface Z.
   a. Integers0
   b. Thing
   c. Undefined
   d. Undefined

53. The _____ of a solid object is the three-dimensional concept of how much space it occupies, often quantified numerically.
   a. Thing
   b. Volume0
   c. Undefined
   d. Undefined

54. In geometry, a _____ is a three-dimensional figure formed by six parallelograms.
   a. Parallelepiped0
   b. Thing
   c. Undefined
   d. Undefined

55. In mathematics and its applications, _____ are used for assigning an n-tuple of numbers or scalars to each point in an n-dimensional space.
   a. Concept
   b. Coordinate systems0
   c. Undefined
   d. Undefined

56. In mathematics, an element x of a ring R is called _____ if there exists some positive integer n such that $x^n = 0$.

Chapter 4. Determinants of Order

　　a. Nilpotent0
　　b. Thing
　　c. Undefined
　　d. Undefined

57. In mathematics, particularly linear algebra, a _____ is a matrix with all its entries being zero.
　　a. Zero matrix0
　　b. Thing
　　c. Undefined
　　d. Undefined

58. In mathematics, _____ is synonymous with perpendicular when used as a simple adjective that is not part of any longer phrase with a standard definition. It means at right angles. It comes from the Greek ἀντί ὀρθός, orthos, meaning "straight", used by Euclid to mean right; and γωνία gonia, meaning angle. Two streets that cross each other at a right angle are _____ to one another.
　　a. Orthogonal0
　　b. Thing
　　c. Undefined
　　d. Undefined

59. In algebra, a _____ is a binomial formed by taking the opposite of the second term of a binomial.
　　a. Thing
　　b. Conjugate0
　　c. Undefined
　　d. Undefined

60. A _____ is a set whose members are members of another set or a set contained within another set.
　　a. Thing
　　b. Subset0
　　c. Undefined
　　d. Undefined

61. The _____ of a ring R is defined to be the smallest positive integer n such that $n\,a = 0$, for all a in R.

Chapter 4. Determinants of Order

a. Thing
b. Characteristic0
c. Undefined
d. Undefined

62. Alexandre-Théophile _____ was a French musician and chemist who worked with Bezout and Lavoisier; his name is now principally associated with determinant theory in mathematics. He was born in Paris, and died there.
a. Vandermonde0
b. Person
c. Undefined
d. Undefined

63. _____ is the state of being greater than any finite real or natural number, however large.
a. Infinite0
b. Thing
c. Undefined
d. Undefined

64. An _____ is a square matrix which has an inverse.
a. Thing
b. Invertible matrix0
c. Undefined
d. Undefined

65. _____ is a collection of objects called vectors that, informally speaking, may be scaled and added.
a. Thing
b. Vector space0
c. Undefined
d. Undefined

66. _____ is a set, with some particular properties and usually some additional structure, such as the operations of addition or multiplication, for instance.

Chapter 4. Determinants of Order

a. Thing
b. Space0
c. Undefined
d. Undefined

67. In combinatorial mathematics, a _____ is an un-ordered collection of unique elements.
a. Concept
b. Combination0
c. Undefined
d. Undefined

68. _____ is one of the basic operations defining a vector space in linear algebra.
a. Scalar multiplication0
b. Thing
c. Undefined
d. Undefined

69. In logic and mathematics, logical _____ is a logical relation that holds between a set T of formulas and a formula B when every model (or interpretation or valuation) of T is also a model of B.
a. Concept
b. Implication0
c. Undefined
d. Undefined

Chapter 5. Eigenvalues and Eigenvectors

1. The word _____ comes from the Latin word linearis, which means created by lines.
   a. Thing
   b. Linear0
   c. Undefined
   d. Undefined

2. In mathematics, a _____ is a rectangular table of numbers or, more generally, a table consisting of abstract quantities that can be added and multiplied.
   a. Matrix0
   b. Thing
   c. Undefined
   d. Undefined

3. _____ is a branch of mathematics concerning the study of structure, relation and quantity.
   a. Algebra0
   b. Concept
   c. Undefined
   d. Undefined

4. A _____ can refer to a line joining two nonadjacent vertices of a polygon or polyhedron, or in some contexts any upward or downward sloping line. .
   a. Thing
   b. Diagonal0
   c. Undefined
   d. Undefined

5. A vector can be thought of as an arrow. It has a length, called its magnitude, and it points in some particular direction. A linear transformation inputs a vector and changes it, usually changing both its magnitude and its direction. An eigenvector of a given linear transformation is a vector which is simply multiplied by a constant called the _____ during that transformation.
   a. Thing
   b. Eigenvalue0
   c. Undefined
   d. Undefined

6. An _____ of a linear transformation is a non-zero vector that is either left unaffected or simply multiplied by a scale factor after the transformation.

a. Eigenvector0
b. Thing
c. Undefined
d. Undefined

7. In mathematics, a _____ (also spelled reflexion) is a map that transforms an object into its mirror image.
a. Reflection0
b. Concept
c. Undefined
d. Undefined

8. _____ is a square matrix in which the entries outside the main diagonal are all zero.
a. Thing
b. Diagonal matrix0
c. Undefined
d. Undefined

9. In physics and in _____ calculus, a spatial _____, or simply _____, is a concept characterized by a magnitude and a direction.
a. Vector0
b. Thing
c. Undefined
d. Undefined

10. _____ is a collection of objects called vectors that, informally speaking, may be scaled and added.
a. Vector space0
b. Thing
c. Undefined
d. Undefined

11. _____ is a set, with some particular properties and usually some additional structure, such as the operations of addition or multiplication, for instance.

a. Thing
b. Space0
c. Undefined
d. Undefined

12. In linear algebra, a square matrix A is called _____ if it is similar to a diagonal matrix, i.e. if there exists an invertible matrix P such that P â˜¯1AP is a diagonal matrix. If V is a finite-dimensional vector space, then a linear map T : V â†' V is called _____ if there exists a basis of V with respect to which T is represented by a diagonal matrix. Diagonalization is the process of finding a corresponding diagonal matrix for a _____ matrix or linear map.
   a. Thing
   b. Diagonalizable0
   c. Undefined
   d. Undefined

13. In mathematics, a set is called _____ if there is a bijection between the set and some set of the form {1, 2, ..., n} where n is a natural number.
   a. Finite0
   b. Thing
   c. Undefined
   d. Undefined

14. In plane geometry, a _____ is a polygon with four equal sides, four right angles, and parallel opposite sides. In algebra, the _____ of a number is that number multiplied by itself.
   a. Square0
   b. Thing
   c. Undefined
   d. Undefined

15. A _____ fraction is a fraction in which the absolute value of the numerator is less than the denominator--hence, the absolute value of the fraction is less than 1.
   a. Proper0
   b. Thing
   c. Undefined
   d. Undefined

16. The _____ of a ring R is defined to be the smallest positive integer n such that n a = 0, for all a in R.

Chapter 5. Eigenvalues and Eigenvectors

   a. Thing
   b. Characteristic0
   c. Undefined
   d. Undefined

17. In linear algebra, real numbers are called scalars and relate to vectors in a vector space through the operation of _____ multiplication, in which a vector can be multiplied by a number to produce another vector.
   a. Thing
   b. Scalar0
   c. Undefined
   d. Undefined

18. In mathematics, a _____ is a statement that can be proved on the basis of explicitly stated or previously agreed assumptions.
   a. Thing
   b. Theorem0
   c. Undefined
   d. Undefined

19. The _____ is a measurement of how a function changes when the values of its inputs change.
   a. Derivative0
   b. Thing
   c. Undefined
   d. Undefined

20. The mathematical concept of a _____ expresses the intuitive idea of deterministic dependence between two quantities, one of which is viewed as primary and the other as secondary. A _____ then is a way to associate a unique output for each input of a specified type, for example, a real number or an element of a given set.
   a. Thing
   b. Function0
   c. Undefined
   d. Undefined

21. In mathematics, a _____ is a demonstration that, assuming certain axioms, some statement is necessarily true.

Chapter 5. Eigenvalues and Eigenvectors

   a. Thing
   b. Proof0
   c. Undefined
   d. Undefined

22. In mathematics, the idea of _____ generalises the concepts of negation, in relation to addition, and reciprocal, in relation to multiplication.
   a. Thing
   b. Inverse element0
   c. Undefined
   d. Undefined

23. In mathematics, a _____ is an expression that is constructed from one or more variables and constants, using only the operations of addition, subtraction, multiplication, and constant positive whole number exponents. is a _____. Note in particular that division by an expression containing a variable is not in general allowed in polynomials. [1]
   a. Thing
   b. Polynomial0
   c. Undefined
   d. Undefined

24. In statistics, a _____ measure is one which is measuring what is supposed to measure.
   a. Thing
   b. Valid0
   c. Undefined
   d. Undefined

25. In mathematics, a _____ is the end result of a division problem. It can also be expressed as the number of times the divisor divides into the dividend.
   a. Thing
   b. Quotient0
   c. Undefined
   d. Undefined

26. In mathematics, a _____ is a constant multiplicative factor of a certain object. The object can be such things as a variable, a vector, a function, etc. For example, the _____ of $9x^2$ is 9.

Chapter 5. Eigenvalues and Eigenvectors

   a. Thing
   b. Coefficient0
   c. Undefined
   d. Undefined

27. In algebra, a _____ is a function depending on n that associates a scalar, $det(A)$, to every $n \times n$ square matrix A.
   a. Thing
   b. Determinant0
   c. Undefined
   d. Undefined

28. In mathematics, science including computer science, linguistics and engineering, an _____ is, generally speaking, an independent variable or input to a function.
   a. Thing
   b. Argument0
   c. Undefined
   d. Undefined

29. In mathematics, there are several meanings of _____ depending on the subject.
   a. Degree0
   b. Thing
   c. Undefined
   d. Undefined

30. In mathematics, a matrix can be thought of as each row or _____ being a vector. Hence, a space formed by row vectors or _____ vectors are said to be a row space or a _____ space.
   a. Column0
   b. Concept
   c. Undefined
   d. Undefined

31. A _____ is a set of numbers that designate location in a given reference system, such as x,y in a planar _____ system or an x,y,z in a three-dimensional _____ system.

a. Coordinate0
b. Thing
c. Undefined
d. Undefined

32. In mathematics, a _____ in elementary terms is any of a variety of different functions from geometry, such as rotations, reflections and translations.
   a. Transformation0
   b. Thing
   c. Undefined
   d. Undefined

33. In mathematics, an _____ on a real vector space is a choice of which ordered bases are "positively" oriented, or right-handed, and which are "negatively" oriented, or left-handed.
   a. Orientation0
   b. Thing
   c. Undefined
   d. Undefined

34. An _____ is an equality that remains true regardless of the values of any variables that appear within it, to distinguish it from an equality which is true under more particular conditions.
   a. Thing
   b. Identity0
   c. Undefined
   d. Undefined

35. In a mathematical proof or a syllogism, a _____ is a statement that is the logical consequence of preceding statements.
   a. Conclusion0
   b. Concept
   c. Undefined
   d. Undefined

36. _____ of a polynomial with real or complex coefficients is a certain expression in the coefficients of the polynomial which is equal to zero if and only if the polynomial has a multiple root i.e. a root with multiplicity greater than one in the complex numbers.

a. Discriminant0
b. Thing
c. Undefined
d. Undefined

37. _____ is the state of being greater than any finite real or natural number, however large.
a. Thing
b. Infinite0
c. Undefined
d. Undefined

38. A _____ is the result of the addition of a set of numbers. The numbers may be natural numbers, complex numbers, matrices, or still more complicated objects. An infinite _____ is a subtle procedure known as a series.
a. Thing
b. Sum0
c. Undefined
d. Undefined

39. _____ is a special kind of square matrix where the entries below or above the main diagonal are zero.
a. Triangular form0
b. Thing
c. Undefined
d. Undefined

40. In linear algebra, the _____ of an n-by-n square matrix A is defined to be the sum of the elements on the main diagonal of A,
a. Trace0
b. Thing
c. Undefined
d. Undefined

41. _____ is a method of mathematical proof typically used to establish that a given statement is true of all natural numbers

Chapter 5. Eigenvalues and Eigenvectors

   a. Mathematical induction0
   b. Thing
   c. Undefined
   d. Undefined

42. A _____ is a mathematical statement which follows easily from a previously proven statement, typically a mathematical theorem.
   a. Thing
   b. Corollary0
   c. Undefined
   d. Undefined

43. Acid _____ ratio measures the ability of a company to use its near cash or quick assets to immediately extinguish its current liabilities.
   a. Test0
   b. Thing
   c. Undefined
   d. Undefined

44. In mathematics, a _____ is the result of multiplying, or an expression that identifies factors to be multiplied.
   a. Thing
   b. Product0
   c. Undefined
   d. Undefined

45. In mathematics, factorization (British English: factorisation) or factoring is the decomposition of an object (for example, a number, a polynomial, or a matrix) into a product of other objects, or _____, which when multiplied together give the original.
   a. Thing
   b. Factors0
   c. Undefined
   d. Undefined

46. _____ Logic is a concept in traditional logic referring to a "type of immediate inference in which from a given proposition another proposition is inferred which has as its subject the predicate of the original proposition and as its predicate the subject of the original proposition (the quality of the proposition being retained)."

Chapter 5. Eigenvalues and Eigenvectors

  a. Concept
  b. Converse0
  c. Undefined
  d. Undefined

47. The _____ of a member of a multiset is how many memberships in the multiset it has.
  a. Thing
  b. Multiplicity0
  c. Undefined
  d. Undefined

48. In mathematics, the _____ (also nullspace) of an operator A is the set of all operands v which solve the equation Av = 0. It is also called the kernel of A.
  a. Thing
  b. Null space0
  c. Undefined
  d. Undefined

49. An _____ of a given transformation is the set of all eigenvectors of that transformation that have the same eigenvalue, together with the zero vector (which has no direction). An _____ is an example of a subspace of a vector space.
  a. Eigenspace0
  b. Thing
  c. Undefined
  d. Undefined

50. In linear algebra and related areas of mathematics, the null vector or _____ is the vector in Euclidean space, all of whose components are zero.
  a. Zero vector0
  b. Thing
  c. Undefined
  d. Undefined

51. In mathematics and the mathematical sciences, a _____ is a fixed, but possibly unspecified, value. This is in contrast to a variable, which is not fixed.

Chapter 5. Eigenvalues and Eigenvectors

a. Constant0
b. Thing
c. Undefined
d. Undefined

52. A _____ is the quantity that defines certain relatively constant characteristics of systems or functions..
a. Parameter0
b. Thing
c. Undefined
d. Undefined

53. A _____ is an equation in which each term is either a constant or the product of a constant times the first power of a variable.
a. Thing
b. Linear equation0
c. Undefined
d. Undefined

54. _____ statistics are statistics that estimate population parameters.
a. Thing
b. Parametric0
c. Undefined
d. Undefined

55. In set theory and other branches of mathematics, the _____ of a collection of sets is the set that contains everything that belongs to any of the sets, but nothing else.
a. Thing
b. Union0
c. Undefined
d. Undefined

56. A _____ is a set whose members are members of another set or a set contained within another set.

a. Thing
b. Subset0
c. Undefined
d. Undefined

57. Equivalence is the condition of being _____ or essentially equal.
a. Equivalent0
b. Thing
c. Undefined
d. Undefined

58. A _____ is a negotiable instrument instructing a financial institution to pay a specific amount of a specific currency from a specific demand account held in the maker/depositor's name with that institution. Both the maker and payee may be natural persons or legal entities.
a. Check0
b. Thing
c. Undefined
d. Undefined

59. In linear algebra, the _____ refers to a matrix consisting of the coefficients of the variables in a set of linear equations.
a. Thing
b. Coefficient matrix0
c. Undefined
d. Undefined

60. Mathematical _____ are the wide variety of ways to capture an abstract mathematical concept or relationship.
a. Thing
b. Representations0
c. Undefined
d. Undefined

61. In mathematics and logic, a _____ proof is a way of showing the truth or falsehood of a given statement by a straightforward combination of established facts, usually existing lemmas and theorems, without making any further assumptions.

Chapter 5. Eigenvalues and Eigenvectors

   a. Thing
   b. Direct0
   c. Undefined
   d. Undefined

62. An _____ is a combination of numbers, operators, grouping symbols and/or free variables and bound variables arranged in a meaningful way which can be evaluated..
   a. Expression0
   b. Thing
   c. Undefined
   d. Undefined

63. A _____ is traditionally an infinitesimally small change in a variable.
   a. Differential0
   b. Thing
   c. Undefined
   d. Undefined

64. A _____ is a mathematical equation for an unknown function of one or several variables which relates the values of the function itself and of its derivatives of various orders.
   a. Thing
   b. Differential equation0
   c. Undefined
   d. Undefined

65. _____ is the property of two events happening at the same time in at least one reference frame.
   a. Thing
   b. Simultaneous0
   c. Undefined
   d. Undefined

66. In mathematics, a _____ is an ordered list of objects. Like a set, it contains members, also called elements or terms, and the number of terms is called the length of the _____. Unlike a set, order matters, and the exact same elements can appear multiple times at different positions in the _____.

Chapter 5. Eigenvalues and Eigenvectors

   a. Thing
   b. Sequence0
   c. Undefined
   d. Undefined

67. In mathematics, a _____ may be described informally as a number that can be given by an infinite decimal representation.
   a. Thing
   b. Real number0
   c. Undefined
   d. Undefined

68. In mathematics, an _____ number is a complex number whose square is a negative real number. They were defined in 1572 by Rafael Bombelli.
   a. Thing
   b. Imaginary0
   c. Undefined
   d. Undefined

69. In mathematics, the _____ of a complex number z, is the second element of the ordered pair of real numbers representing z, i.e. if z = (x,y), or equivalently, z = x + iy, then the _____ of z is y.
   a. Thing
   b. Imaginary part0
   c. Undefined
   d. Undefined

70. _____ is the logarithm to the base e, where e is an irrational constant approximately equal to 2.718281828459.
   a. Thing
   b. Natural logarithm0
   c. Undefined
   d. Undefined

71. In mathematics, a _____ of a number x is the exponent y of the power by such that $x = b^y$. The value used for the base b must be neither 0 nor 1, nor a root of 1 in the case of the extension to complex numbers, and is typically 10, e, or 2.

Chapter 5. Eigenvalues and Eigenvectors

   a. Thing
   b. Logarithm0
   c. Undefined
   d. Undefined

72. An _____ is a square matrix which has an inverse.
   a. Thing
   b. Invertible matrix0
   c. Undefined
   d. Undefined

73. In classical geometry, a _____ of a circle or sphere is any line segment from its center to its boundary. By extension, the _____ of a circle or sphere is the length of any such segment. The _____ is half the diameter. In science and engineering the term _____ of curvature is commonly used as a synonym for _____.
   a. Thing
   b. Radius0
   c. Undefined
   d. Undefined

74. In mathematics, the _____ of a coordinate system is the point where the axes of the system intersect.
   a. Thing
   b. Origin0
   c. Undefined
   d. Undefined

75. _____ is the fee paid on borrowed money.
   a. Interest0
   b. Thing
   c. Undefined
   d. Undefined

76. In mathematics, a _____ is a number in the form of a + bi where a and b are real numbers, and i is the imaginary unit, with the property i 2 = −1. The real number a is called the real part of the _____, and the real number b is the imaginary part.

Chapter 5. Eigenvalues and Eigenvectors

   a. Thing
   b. Complex number0
   c. Undefined
   d. Undefined

77. _____ is the chance that something is likely to happen or be the case.
   a. Thing
   b. Probability0
   c. Undefined
   d. Undefined

78. The _____ integers are all the integers from zero on upwards.
   a. Thing
   b. Nonnegative0
   c. Undefined
   d. Undefined

79. A _____ is a deliberate process for transforming one or more inputs into one or more results.
   a. Thing
   b. Calculation0
   c. Undefined
   d. Undefined

80. In mathematics, a _____ describes the transitions of a Markov chain. It has found use in probability theory, statistics and linear algebra, as well as computer science.
   a. Thing
   b. Stochastic matrix0
   c. Undefined
   d. Undefined

81. _____ is a special mathematical relationship between two quantities.Two quantities are called proportional if they vary in such a way that one of the quantities is a constant multiple of the other, or equivalently if they have a constant ratio.

Chapter 5. Eigenvalues and Eigenvectors

a. Proportionality0
b. Thing
c. Undefined
d. Undefined

82. _____ (or proportionality) are two quantities that vary in such a way that one of the quatities is a constant multiple of the other, or equivalently if they have a constant ratio.
a. Proportions0
b. Thing
c. Undefined
d. Undefined

83. In sociology and biology a _____ is the collection of people or organisms of a particular species living in a given geographic area or space, usually measured by a census.
a. Population0
b. Thing
c. Undefined
d. Undefined

84. _____ is an m × 1 matrix, i.e. a matrix consisting of a single column of m elements.
a. Column vector0
b. Thing
c. Undefined
d. Undefined

85. An _____ or member of a set is an object that when collected together make up the set.
a. Element0
b. Thing
c. Undefined
d. Undefined

86. In mathematics, the _____ , or members of a set or more generally a class are all those objects which when collected together make up the set or class.

Chapter 5. Eigenvalues and Eigenvectors

   a. Thing
   b. Elements0
   c. Undefined
   d. Undefined

87. _____, from the Greek "stochos" or "aim, guess", means of, relating to, or characterized by conjecture and randomness. A _____ process is one whose behavior is non-deterministic in that a state does not fully determine its next state.
   a. Stochastic0
   b. Thing
   c. Undefined
   d. Undefined

88. In elementary algebra, an _____ is a set that contains every real number between two indicated numbers and may contain the two numbers themselves.
   a. Interval0
   b. Thing
   c. Undefined
   d. Undefined

89. A _____ is a series of states of a system that has the Markov property. At each time the system may have changed from the state it was in the moment before, or it may have stayed in the same state.
   a. Markov chain0
   b. Thing
   c. Undefined
   d. Undefined

90. _____ is a synonym for information.
   a. Data0
   b. Thing
   c. Undefined
   d. Undefined

91. _____ has many meanings, most of which simply .

Chapter 5. Eigenvalues and Eigenvectors

   a. Thing
   b. Power0
   c. Undefined
   d. Undefined

92. In mathematics, a _____ function in the sense of algebraic geometry is an everywhere-defined, polynomial function on an algebraic variety V with values in the field K over which V is defined.
   a. Regular0
   b. Thing
   c. Undefined
   d. Undefined

93. The _____ of a mathematical object is its size: a property by which it can be larger or smaller than other objects of the same kind; in technical terms, an ordering of the class of objects to which it belongs.
   a. Thing
   b. Magnitude0
   c. Undefined
   d. Undefined

94. _____ is the study of terms and their use — of words and compound words that are used in specific contexts.
   a. Terminology0
   b. Thing
   c. Undefined
   d. Undefined

95. In mathematics, the _____ (or modulus) of a real number is its numerical value without regard to its sign.
   a. Absolute value0
   b. Thing
   c. Undefined
   d. Undefined

96. In mathematics, especially in order theory, an _____ of a subset S of some partially ordered set is an element of P which is greater than or equal to every element of S.

Chapter 5. Eigenvalues and Eigenvectors

a. Upper bound0
b. Thing
c. Undefined
d. Undefined

97. Two mathematical objects are equal if and only if they are precisely the same in every way. This defines a binary relation, _____, denoted by the sign of _____ "=" in such a way that the statement "x = y" means that x and y are equal.
a. Equality0
b. Thing
c. Undefined
d. Undefined

98. In mathematics, an _____ is a statement about the relative size or order of two objects.
a. Thing
b. Inequality0
c. Undefined
d. Undefined

99. A _____ of a number is the product of that number with any integer.
a. Multiple0
b. Thing
c. Undefined
d. Undefined

100. In common philosophical language, a proposition or _____, is the content of an assertion, that is, it is true-or-false and defined by the meaning of a particular piece of language.
a. Concept
b. Statement0
c. Undefined
d. Undefined

101. In mathematical analysis, _____ are objects which generalize functions and probability distributions.

Chapter 5. Eigenvalues and Eigenvectors

a. Distribution0
b. Thing
c. Undefined
d. Undefined

102. Initial objects are also called _____, and terminal objects are also called final.
a. Thing
b. Coterminal0
c. Undefined
d. Undefined

103. _____ is a kind of property which exists as magnitude or multitude. It is among the basic classes of things along with quality, substance, change, and relation.
a. Amount0
b. Thing
c. Undefined
d. Undefined

104. In mathematics, particularly linear algebra, a _____ is a matrix with all its entries being zero.
a. Thing
b. Zero matrix0
c. Undefined
d. Undefined

105. A _____ is an abstract model that uses mathematical language to describe the behavior of a system. Eykhoff defined a _____ as 'a representation of the essential aspects of an existing system which presents knowledge of that system in usable form'.
a. Mathematical model0
b. Thing
c. Undefined
d. Undefined

106. The word _____ comes from the 15th Century Latin word discretus which means separate.

Chapter 5. Eigenvalues and Eigenvectors

   a. Discrete0
   b. Thing
   c. Undefined
   d. Undefined

107. In the scientific method, an _____ (Latin: ex-+-periri, "of (or from) trying"), is a set of actions and observations, performed in the context of solving a particular problem or question, in order to support or falsify a hypothesis or research concerning phenomena.
   a. Experiment0
   b. Thing
   c. Undefined
   d. Undefined

108. In combinatorial mathematics, a _____ is an un-ordered collection of unique elements.
   a. Concept
   b. Combination0
   c. Undefined
   d. Undefined

109. _____ the expected value of a random variable displays the average or central value of the variable. It is a summary value of the distribution of the variable.
   a. Thing
   b. Determining0
   c. Undefined
   d. Undefined

110. A _____ is the sum of the elements of a sequence.
   a. Series0
   b. Thing
   c. Undefined
   d. Undefined

111. _____ is often represented as the sum of a sequence of terms.

Chapter 5. Eigenvalues and Eigenvectors

  a. Thing
  b. Infinite series0
  c. Undefined
  d. Undefined

112. A _____, is a symbolized depiction of space which highlights relations between components of that space. Most usually a _____ is a two-dimensional, geometrically accurate representation of a three-dimensional space.
  a. Thing
  b. Map0
  c. Undefined
  d. Undefined

113. In mathematics, an _____ is something that does not change under a set of transformations. The property of being an _____ is invariance.
  a. Invariant0
  b. Thing
  c. Undefined
  d. Undefined

114. In mathematics, a _____ of a k-place relation $L \subseteq X_1 \times \ldots \times X_k$ is one of the sets X_j, $1 \leq j \leq k$. In the special case where k = 2 and $L \subseteq X_1 \times X_2$ is a function $L : X_1 \to X_2$, it is conventional to refer to X_1 as the _____ of the function and to refer to X_2 as the codomain of the function.
  a. Thing
  b. Domain0
  c. Undefined
  d. Undefined

115. Mathematical _____ is used to represent ideas.
  a. Notation0
  b. Thing
  c. Undefined
  d. Undefined

116. The _____, the average in everyday English, which is also called the arithmetic _____ (and is distinguished from the geometric _____ or harmonic _____). The average is also called the sample _____. The expected value of a random variable, which is also called the population _____.

Chapter 5. Eigenvalues and Eigenvectors

  a. Mean0
  b. Thing
  c. Undefined
  d. Undefined

117. A _____ consists either of a suggested explanation for a phenomenon or of a reasoned proposal suggesting a possible correlation between multiple phenomena.
  a. Hypothesis0
  b. Thing
  c. Undefined
  d. Undefined

118. In mathematics, if G is a group, H a subgroup of G, and g an element of G, then, gH = {gh : h an element of H } is a left _____ of H in G, and Hg = {hg : h an element of H} is a right _____ of H in G.
  a. Thing
  b. Coset0
  c. Undefined
  d. Undefined

119. In mathematics, a _____ of a positive integer n is a way of writing n as a sum of positive integers.
  a. Composition0
  b. Thing
  c. Undefined
  d. Undefined

Chapter 6. Inner Product Spaces

1. In mathematics, a _____ is the result of multiplying, or an expression that identifies factors to be multiplied.
   a. Thing
   b. Product0
   c. Undefined
   d. Undefined

2. In mathematics, a _____ is any one of several different types of functions, mappings, operations, or transformations.
   a. Thing
   b. Projection0
   c. Undefined
   d. Undefined

3. In mathematics, and in particular linear algebra, the _____ A + of an m x n matrix A is a generalization of the inverse matrix. More precisely, this article talks about the Moore-Penrose _____, which was independently described by E. H. Moore in 1920 and Roger Penrose in 1955. Earlier, Fredholm had introduced the concept of a _____ of integral operators in 1903.
   a. Pseudoinverse0
   b. Thing
   c. Undefined
   d. Undefined

4. In mathematics, a _____ is a homogeneous polynomial of degree two in a number of variables.
   a. Quadratic form0
   b. Thing
   c. Undefined
   d. Undefined

5. In mathematics, a _____ is the end result of a division problem. It can also be expressed as the number of times the divisor divides into the dividend.
   a. Quotient0
   b. Thing
   c. Undefined
   d. Undefined

6. In mathematics, for a given complex Hermitian matrix A and nonzero vector x, the _____ R is defined as: x^*Ax/x^*x

Chapter 6. Inner Product Spaces

   a. Thing
   b. Rayleigh quotient0
   c. Undefined
   d. Undefined

7. _____ is a set, with some particular properties and usually some additional structure, such as the operations of addition or multiplication, for instance.
   a. Space0
   b. Thing
   c. Undefined
   d. Undefined

8. In mathematics, particularly linear algebra and functional analysis, the _____ is any of a number of results about linear operators or about matrices. In broad terms the _____ provides conditions under which an operator or a matrix can be diagonalized . This concept of diagonalization is relatively straightforward for operators on finite-dimensional spaces, but requires some modification for operators on infinite-dimensional spaces. In general, the _____ identifies a class of linear operators that can be modelled by multiplication operators, which are as simple as one can hope to find.
   a. Spectral theorem0
   b. Thing
   c. Undefined
   d. Undefined

9. _____ refers to the reduction of the body of a formerly living organism into simpler forms of matter.
   a. Decomposing0
   b. Thing
   c. Undefined
   d. Undefined

10. In mathematics, _____ is synonymous with perpendicular when used as a simple adjective that is not part of any longer phrase with a standard definition. It means at right angles. It comes from the Greek á½€ἴ Î¸ÏŒÏ, orthos, meaning "straight", used by Euclid to mean right; and Î³Ï‰Î½Î¯Î± gonia, meaning angle. Two streets that cross each other at a right angle are _____ to one another.
   a. Thing
   b. Orthogonal0
   c. Undefined
   d. Undefined

11. In linear algebra, _____ means the following: We start with a linearly independent set of vectors $\{v_1,...,v_k\}$ in an inner product space and we want to find a set of pairwise orthogonal vectors $\{u_1,...,u_k\}$ that generate the same subspace as the vectors $v_1,...,v_k$. In other words, every vector in the new set is orthogonal to every other vector in the new set; and the new set and the old set have the same linear span.
   a. Thing
   b. Orthogonalization0
   c. Undefined
   d. Undefined

12. The word _____ comes from the Latin word linearis, which means created by lines.
   a. Thing
   b. Linear0
   c. Undefined
   d. Undefined

13. The _____ of a mathematical object is its size: a property by which it can be larger or smaller than other objects of the same kind; in technical terms, an ordering of the class of objects to which it belongs.
   a. Thing
   b. Magnitude0
   c. Undefined
   d. Undefined

14. In mathematics, a _____ is a rectangular table of numbers or, more generally, a table consisting of abstract quantities that can be added and multiplied.
   a. Matrix0
   b. Thing
   c. Undefined
   d. Undefined

15. _____ is the estimation of a physical quantity such as distance, energy, temperature, or time.
   a. Thing
   b. Measurement0
   c. Undefined
   d. Undefined

Chapter 6. Inner Product Spaces

16. In mathematics, a _____ is a statement that can be proved on the basis of explicitly stated or previously agreed assumptions.
   a. Theorem0
   b. Thing
   c. Undefined
   d. Undefined

17. In set theory and other branches of mathematics, two kinds of complements are defined, the relative _____ and the absolute _____.
   a. Complement0
   b. Thing
   c. Undefined
   d. Undefined

18. In physics and in _____ calculus, a spatial _____, or simply _____, is a concept characterized by a magnitude and a direction.
   a. Vector0
   b. Thing
   c. Undefined
   d. Undefined

19. _____ is a collection of objects called vectors that, informally speaking, may be scaled and added.
   a. Thing
   b. Vector space0
   c. Undefined
   d. Undefined

20. An _____ is a collection of two not necessarily distinct objects, one of which is distinguished as the first coordinate and the other as the second coordinate.
   a. Ordered pair0
   b. Thing
   c. Undefined
   d. Undefined

Chapter 6. Inner Product Spaces

21. The mathematical concept of a _____ expresses the intuitive idea of deterministic dependence between two quantities, one of which is viewed as primary and the other as secondary. A _____ then is a way to associate a unique output for each input of a specified type, for example, a real number or an element of a given set.
   a. Function0
   b. Thing
   c. Undefined
   d. Undefined

22. In mathematics, in the field of group theory, a _____ of a group is a quasisimple subnormal subgroup.
   a. Concept
   b. Component0
   c. Undefined
   d. Undefined

23. In mathematics, the _____, also known as the scalar product, is a binary operation which takes two vectors over the real numbers R and returns a real-valued scalar quantity. It is the standard inner product of the Euclidean space.
   a. Dot product0
   b. Thing
   c. Undefined
   d. Undefined

24. A _____ function is a function for which, intuitively, small changes in the input result in small changes in the output.
   a. Continuous0
   b. Event
   c. Undefined
   d. Undefined

25. The _____ of a function is an extension of the concept of a sum, and are identified or found through the use of integration.
   a. Thing
   b. Integral0
   c. Undefined
   d. Undefined

Chapter 6. Inner Product Spaces

26. In mathematical analysis and related areas of mathematics, a set is called _____, if it is, in a certain sense, of finite size.
   a. Thing
   b. Bounded0
   c. Undefined
   d. Undefined

27. In linear algebra, the _____ of a matrix A is another matrix AT
   a. Thing
   b. Transpose0
   c. Undefined
   d. Undefined

28. In algebra, a _____ is a binomial formed by taking the opposite of the second term of a binomial.
   a. Thing
   b. Conjugate0
   c. Undefined
   d. Undefined

29. In elementary algebra, an _____ is a set that contains every real number between two indicated numbers and may contain the two numbers themselves.
   a. Interval0
   b. Thing
   c. Undefined
   d. Undefined

30. In mathematics and the mathematical sciences, a _____ is a fixed, but possibly unspecified, value. This is in contrast to a variable, which is not fixed.
   a. Constant0
   b. Thing
   c. Undefined
   d. Undefined

31. _____ is a process of combining or accumulating. It may also refer to:

a. Thing
b. Integration0
c. Undefined
d. Undefined

32. In mathematics, a _____ is a demonstration that, assuming certain axioms, some statement is necessarily true.
a. Proof0
b. Thing
c. Undefined
d. Undefined

33. Mathematical _____ are demonstrations that, assuming certain axioms, some statement is necessarily true.
a. Thing
b. Proofs0
c. Undefined
d. Undefined

34. In mathematics, an _____ is a statement about the relative size or order of two objects.
a. Thing
b. Inequality0
c. Undefined
d. Undefined

35. The _____ is a useful inequality encountered in many different settings, such as linear algebra applied to vectors, in analysis applied to infinite series and integration of products, and in probability theory, applied to variances and covariances.
a. Buniakowsky inequality0
b. Thing
c. Undefined
d. Undefined

36. A _____ is one of the basic shapes of geometry: a polygon with three vertices and three sides which are straight line segments.

Chapter 6. Inner Product Spaces

    a. Triangle0
    b. Thing
    c. Undefined
    d. Undefined

37. _____ is the theorem stating that for any triangle, the measure of a given side must be less than the sum of the other two sides but greater than the difference between the two sides.
    a. Triangle inequality0
    b. Thing
    c. Undefined
    d. Undefined

38. A _____ is a set whose members are members of another set or a set contained within another set.
    a. Subset0
    b. Thing
    c. Undefined
    d. Undefined

39. In geometry, two lines or planes if one falls on the other in such a way as to create congruent adjacent angles. The term may be used as a noun or adjective. Thus, referring to Figure 1, the line AB is the _____ to CD through the point B.
    a. Perpendicular0
    b. Thing
    c. Undefined
    d. Undefined

40. _____ in a normed vector space is a vector whose length, or magnitude is 1.
    a. Unit vector0
    b. Thing
    c. Undefined
    d. Undefined

41. In linear algebra, two vectors in an inner product space are _____ if they are orthogonal (their inner product is 0) and both of unit length (the norm of each is 1). A set of vectors which is pairwise _____ (any two vectors in it are _____) is called an _____ set. A basis which forms an _____ set is called an _____ basis.

Chapter 6. Inner Product Spaces

   a. Thing
   b. Orthonormal0
   c. Undefined
   d. Undefined

42. In mathematics, the multiplicative inverse of a number x, denoted 1/x or x^{-1}, is the number which, when multiplied by x, yields 1. The multiplicative inverse of x is also called the _____ of x.
   a. Thing
   b. Reciprocal0
   c. Undefined
   d. Undefined

43. In mathematics, a _____ may be described informally as a number that can be given by an infinite decimal representation.
   a. Real number0
   b. Thing
   c. Undefined
   d. Undefined

44. In mathematics, the conjugate _____ or adjoint matrix of an m-by-n matrix A with complex entries is the n-by-m matrix A* obtained from A by taking the transpose and then taking the complex conjugate of each entry.
   a. Thing
   b. Pairs0
   c. Undefined
   d. Undefined

45. In linear algebra, real numbers are called scalars and relate to vectors in a vector space through the operation of _____ multiplication, in which a vector can be multiplied by a number to produce another vector.
   a. Scalar0
   b. Thing
   c. Undefined
   d. Undefined

46. In mathematics, a _____ is a number in the form of a + bi where a and b are real numbers, and i is the imaginary unit, with the property $i^2 = -1$. The real number a is called the real part of the _____, and the real number b is the imaginary part.

a. Thing
b. Complex number0
c. Undefined
d. Undefined

47. In mathematics, a set is called _____ if there is a bijection between the set and some set of the form {1, 2, ..., n} where n is a natural number.
a. Thing
b. Finite0
c. Undefined
d. Undefined

48. In plane geometry, a _____ is a polygon with four equal sides, four right angles, and parallel opposite sides. In algebra, the _____ of a number is that number multiplied by itself.
a. Square0
b. Thing
c. Undefined
d. Undefined

49. _____, a field in mathematics, is the study of how functions change when their inputs change. The primary object of study in _____ is the derivative.
a. Thing
b. Differential calculus0
c. Undefined
d. Undefined

50. A _____ of a number is the product of that number with any integer.
a. Thing
b. Multiple0
c. Undefined
d. Undefined

51. An _____ is an equality that remains true regardless of the values of any variables that appear within it, to distinguish it from an equality which is true under more particular conditions.

Chapter 6. Inner Product Spaces

    a. Thing
    b. Identity0
    c. Undefined
    d. Undefined

52. Two mathematical objects are equal if and only if they are precisely the same in every way. This defines a binary relation, _____, denoted by the sign of _____ "=" in such a way that the statement "x = y" means that x and y are equal.
    a. Equality0
    b. Thing
    c. Undefined
    d. Undefined

53. In mathematics, the _____ of a complex number z, is the first element of the ordered pair of real numbers representing z, i.e. if z = (x,y), or equivalently, z = x + iy, then the _____ of z is x. It is denoted by Re{z} . The complex function which maps z to the _____ of z is not holomorphic.
    a. Thing
    b. Real part0
    c. Undefined
    d. Undefined

54. In functional analysis and related areas of mathematics the _____ set of a given subset of a vector space is a certain set in the dual space.
    a. Polar0
    b. Thing
    c. Undefined
    d. Undefined

55. _____ is the state of being greater than any finite real or natural number, however large.
    a. Thing
    b. Infinite0
    c. Undefined
    d. Undefined

56. In mathematics, a _____ number is a number which can be expressed as a ratio of two integers. Non-integer _____ numbers (commonly called fractions) are usually written as the vulgar fraction a / b, where b is not zero.

a. Thing
b. Rational0
c. Undefined
d. Undefined

57. A _____ is a four-sided plane figure that has two sets of opposite parallel sides.
a. Parallelogram0
b. Concept
c. Undefined
d. Undefined

58. A _____ is a mathematical statement which follows easily from a previously proven statement, typically a mathematical theorem.
a. Corollary0
b. Thing
c. Undefined
d. Undefined

59. In mathematics, a _____ is a constant multiplicative factor of a certain object. The object can be such things as a variable, a vector, a function, etc. For example, the _____ of $9x^2$ is 9.
a. Thing
b. Coefficient0
c. Undefined
d. Undefined

60. In combinatorial mathematics, a _____ is an un-ordered collection of unique elements.
a. Concept
b. Combination0
c. Undefined
d. Undefined

61. _____ consists either of a suggested explanation for a phenomenon or of a reasoned proposal suggesting a possible correlation between multiple phenomena.

Chapter 6. Inner Product Spaces

   a. Hypotheses0
   b. Event
   c. Undefined
   d. Undefined

62. A _____ is a negotiable instrument instructing a financial institution to pay a specific amount of a specific currency from a specific demand account held in the maker/depositor's name with that institution. Both the maker and payee may be natural persons or legal entities.
   a. Check0
   b. Thing
   c. Undefined
   d. Undefined

63. _____ is a method of mathematical proof typically used to establish that a given statement is true of all natural numbers
   a. Mathematical induction0
   b. Thing
   c. Undefined
   d. Undefined

64. An _____ or member of a set is an object that when collected together make up the set.
   a. Element0
   b. Thing
   c. Undefined
   d. Undefined

65. In mathematics, the _____ , or members of a set or more generally a class are all those objects which when collected together make up the set or class.
   a. Thing
   b. Elements0
   c. Undefined
   d. Undefined

66. In mathematics, a _____ is an expression that is constructed from one or more variables and constants, using only the operations of addition, subtraction, multiplication, and constant positive whole number exponents. is a _____. Note in particular that division by an expression containing a variable is not in general allowed in polynomials. [1]

Chapter 6. Inner Product Spaces

a. Thing
b. Polynomial0
c. Undefined
d. Undefined

67. A _____ is the part of the dividend that is left over when the dividend is not evenly divisible by the divisor.
a. Thing
b. Remainder0
c. Undefined
d. Undefined

68. _____ is the study of terms and their use — of words and compound words that are used in specific contexts.
a. Terminology0
b. Thing
c. Undefined
d. Undefined

69. Mathematical _____ is used to represent ideas.
a. Thing
b. Notation0
c. Undefined
d. Undefined

70. In regression analysis, _____, also known as ordinary _____ analysis is a method for linear regression that determines the values of unknown quantities in a statistical model by minimizing the sum of the residuals difference between the predicted and observed values squared.
a. Least squares0
b. Thing
c. Undefined
d. Undefined

71. In mathematics, a _____ is an ordered list of objects. Like a set, it contains members, also called elements or terms, and the number of terms is called the length of the _____. Unlike a set, order matters, and the exact same elements can appear multiple times at different positions in the _____.

Chapter 6. Inner Product Spaces

a. Thing
b. Sequence0
c. Undefined
d. Undefined

72. The _____ are the only integral domain whose positive elements are well-ordered, and in which order is preserved by addition. Like the natural numbers, the _____ form a countably infinite set. The set of all _____ is usually denoted in mathematics by a boldface Z .

a. Integers0
b. Thing
c. Undefined
d. Undefined

73. _____ is bother the congnitive process of transferring information from a particular subject , and a linguistic expression corresponding to such a process.

a. Analogy0
b. Thing
c. Undefined
d. Undefined

74. In mathematics, a _____ in elementary terms is any of a variety of different functions from geometry, such as rotations, reflections and translations.

a. Thing
b. Transformation0
c. Undefined
d. Undefined

75. In mathematics, a linear map also called a _____ or linear operator is a function between two vector spaces that preserves the operations of vector addition and scalar multiplication.

a. Linear transformation0
b. Thing
c. Undefined
d. Undefined

76. _____ is a synonym for information.

Chapter 6. Inner Product Spaces

   a. Thing
   b. Data0
   c. Undefined
   d. Undefined

77. A _____ is a first degree polynomial mathematical function of the form: f(x) = mx + b where m and b are real constants and x is a real variable.
   a. Linear function0
   b. Thing
   c. Undefined
   d. Undefined

78. In mathematics, there are several meanings of _____ depending on the subject.
   a. Degree0
   b. Thing
   c. Undefined
   d. Undefined

79. The easiest _____ prime numbers resides in the use of the Sieve of Eratosthenes, an algorithm that discovers all prime numbers to a specified integer.
   a. Method for finding0
   b. Thing
   c. Undefined
   d. Undefined

80. In mathematics, a matrix can be thought of as each row or _____ being a vector. Hence, a space formed by row vectors or _____ vectors are said to be a row space or a _____ space.
   a. Column0
   b. Concept
   c. Undefined
   d. Undefined

81. _____ is an m × 1 matrix, i.e. a matrix consisting of a single column of m elements.

Chapter 6. Inner Product Spaces

a. Column vector0
b. Thing
c. Undefined
d. Undefined

82. In mathematics, the idea of _____ generalises the concepts of negation, in relation to addition, and reciprocal, in relation to multiplication.
   a. Inverse element0
   b. Thing
   c. Undefined
   d. Undefined

83. A _____ is an equation in which each term is either a constant or the product of a constant times the first power of a variable.
   a. Linear equation0
   b. Thing
   c. Undefined
   d. Undefined

84. A _____ can refer to a line joining two nonadjacent vertices of a polygon or polyhedron, or in some contexts any upward or downward sloping line. .
   a. Thing
   b. Diagonal0
   c. Undefined
   d. Undefined

85. _____ is a square matrix in which the entries outside the main diagonal are all zero.
   a. Diagonal matrix0
   b. Thing
   c. Undefined
   d. Undefined

86. A _____ is a polynomial function of the form $f(x) = ax^2 + bx + c$, where a, b, c are real numbers and a , 0.

Chapter 6. Inner Product Spaces

   a. Quadratic function0
   b. Event
   c. Undefined
   d. Undefined

87. _____, Greek for "knowledge of nature," is the branch of science concerned with the discovery and characterization of universal laws which govern matter, energy, space, and time.
   a. Thing
   b. Physics0
   c. Undefined
   d. Undefined

88. In physics, _____ is an influence that may cause an object to accelerate. It may be experienced as a lift, a push, or a pull. The actual acceleration of the body is determined by the vector sum of all forces acting on it, known as net _____ or resultant _____.
   a. Force0
   b. Thing
   c. Undefined
   d. Undefined

89. _____ of a function of several variables is its derivative with respect to one of those variables with the others held constant as opposed to the total derivative, in which all variables are allowed to vary.
   a. Thing
   b. Partial derivative0
   c. Undefined
   d. Undefined

90. The _____ is a measurement of how a function changes when the values of its inputs change.
   a. Thing
   b. Derivative0
   c. Undefined
   d. Undefined

91. In geometry, the _____ of an object is a point in some sense in the middle of the object.

Chapter 6. Inner Product Spaces

a. Center0
b. Thing
c. Undefined
d. Undefined

92. In physics, the _____ of a system of particles is a specific point at which, for many purposes, the system's mass behaves as if it were concentrated.
a. Thing
b. Center of mass0
c. Undefined
d. Undefined

93. _____ is the property of a physical object that quantifies the amount of matter and energy it is equivalent to.
a. Mass0
b. Thing
c. Undefined
d. Undefined

94. A _____ is the sum of the elements of a sequence.
a. Thing
b. Series0
c. Undefined
d. Undefined

95. _____ is often represented as the sum of a sequence of terms.
a. Thing
b. Infinite series0
c. Undefined
d. Undefined

96. An _____ of a linear transformation is a non-zero vector that is either left unaffected or simply multiplied by a scale factor after the transformation.

Chapter 6. Inner Product Spaces

a. Eigenvector0
b. Thing
c. Undefined
d. Undefined

97. In linear algebra, a square matrix A is called _____ if it is similar to a diagonal matrix, i.e. if there exists an invertible matrix P such that P ⁻¹AP is a diagonal matrix. If V is a finite-dimensional vector space, then a linear map T : V → V is called _____ if there exists a basis of V with respect to which T is represented by a diagonal matrix. Diagonalization is the process of finding a corresponding diagonal matrix for a _____ matrix or linear map.
a. Thing
b. Diagonalizable0
c. Undefined
d. Undefined

98. In mathematics, factorization (British English: factorisation) or factoring is the decomposition of an object (for example, a number, a polynomial, or a matrix) into a product of other objects, or _____, which when multiplied together give the original.
a. Thing
b. Factors0
c. Undefined
d. Undefined

99. The _____ of a ring R is defined to be the smallest positive integer n such that n a = 0, for all a in R.
a. Thing
b. Characteristic0
c. Undefined
d. Undefined

100. A _____ consists either of a suggested explanation for a phenomenon or of a reasoned proposal suggesting a possible correlation between multiple phenomena.
a. Hypothesis0
b. Thing
c. Undefined
d. Undefined

Chapter 6. Inner Product Spaces

101. A _____ is a movement of an object in a circular motion. A two-dimensional object rotates around a center (or point) of _____. A three-dimensional object rotates around a line called an axis. If the axis of _____ is within the body, the body is said to rotate upon itself, or spin—which implies relative speed and perhaps free-movement with angular momentum. A circular motion about an external point, e.g. the Earth about the Sun, is called an orbit or more properly an orbital revolution.
   a. Thing
   b. Rotation0
   c. Undefined
   d. Undefined

102. A vector can be thought of as an arrow. It has a length, called its magnitude, and it points in some particular direction. A linear transformation inputs a vector and changes it, usually changing both its magnitude and its direction. An eigenvector of a given linear transformation is a vector which is simply multiplied by a constant called the _____ during that transformation.
   a. Eigenvalue0
   b. Thing
   c. Undefined
   d. Undefined

103. _____ is a branch of mathematics concerning the study of structure, relation and quantity.
   a. Concept
   b. Algebra0
   c. Undefined
   d. Undefined

104. In number theory, the _____ of arithmetic (or unique factorization theorem) states that every natural number greater than 1 can be written as a unique product of prime numbers.
   a. Fundamental theorem0
   b. Concept
   c. Undefined
   d. Undefined

105. _____ states that every non-zero single-variable polynomial, with complex coefficients, has exactly as many complex roots as its degree, if repeated roots are counted up to their multiplicity.

a. Fundamental theorem of algebra0
b. Thing
c. Undefined
d. Undefined

106. _____ is a mathematical science pertaining to the collection, analysis, interpretation or explanation, and presentation of data. It is applicable to a wide variety of academic disciplines, from the physical and social sciences to the humanities.
a. Statistics0
b. Thing
c. Undefined
d. Undefined

107. An _____ of a given transformation is the set of all eigenvectors of that transformation that have the same eigenvalue, together with the zero vector (which has no direction). An _____ is an example of a subspace of a vector space.
a. Eigenspace0
b. Thing
c. Undefined
d. Undefined

108. _____ Logic is a concept in traditional logic referring to a "type of immediate inference in which from a given proposition another proposition is inferred which has as its subject the predicate of the original proposition and as its predicate the subject of the original proposition (the quality of the proposition being retained)."
a. Converse0
b. Concept
c. Undefined
d. Undefined

109. In mathematics, science including computer science, linguistics and engineering, an _____ is, generally speaking, an independent variable or input to a function.
a. Thing
b. Argument0
c. Undefined
d. Undefined

Chapter 6. Inner Product Spaces

110. _____ is a special kind of square matrix where the entries below or above the main diagonal are zero.
a. Thing
b. Triangular form0
c. Undefined
d. Undefined

111. In mathematics, an _____, isometric isomorphism or congruence mapping is a distance-preserving isomorphism between metric spaces.
a. Thing
b. Isometry0
c. Undefined
d. Undefined

112. In mathematics, a _____ (also spelled reflexion) is a map that transforms an object into its mirror image.
a. Reflection0
b. Concept
c. Undefined
d. Undefined

113. Equivalence is the condition of being _____ or essentially equal.
a. Thing
b. Equivalent0
c. Undefined
d. Undefined

114. In mathematics, the _____ (or modulus) of a real number is its numerical value without regard to its sign.
a. Thing
b. Absolute value0
c. Undefined
d. Undefined

115. In mathematics, the _____ of a coordinate system is the point where the axes of the system intersect.

a. Origin0
b. Thing
c. Undefined
d. Undefined

116. In mathematics, a _____ is a two-dimensional manifold or surface that is perfectly flat.
a. Plane0
b. Thing
c. Undefined
d. Undefined

117. In mathematics, suppose C is a collection of mathematical objects . Then we say that C is _____ if every c ⸴ C is uniquely determined by less information about c than one would expect.
a. Rigid0
b. Thing
c. Undefined
d. Undefined

118. In Euclidean mathematics, _____ consists of a transformation of the plane or space, which preserves distance and angles.
a. Rigid motion0
b. Thing
c. Undefined
d. Undefined

119. In Euclidean geometry, a _____ is moving every point a constant distance in a specified direction.
a. Translation0
b. Concept
c. Undefined
d. Undefined

120. A _____ number is a positive integer which has a positive divisor other than one or itself.

Chapter 6. Inner Product Spaces

a. Composite0
b. Thing
c. Undefined
d. Undefined

121. In mathematics, a _____ section is a curve that can be formed by intersecting a cone with a plane.
a. Conic0
b. Thing
c. Undefined
d. Undefined

122. _____ is a technique used in algebra to solve quadratic equations, in analytic geometry for determining the shapes of graphs, and in calculus for computing integrals, including, but hardly limited to, the integrals that define Laplace transforms. The essential objective is to reduce a quadratic polynomial in a variable in an equation or expression to a squared polynomial of linear order. This can reduce an equation or integral to one that is more easily solved or evaluated.
a. Completing the square0
b. Thing
c. Undefined
d. Undefined

123. A _____ is a set of numbers that designate location in a given reference system, such as x,y in a planar _____ system or an x,y,z in a three-dimensional _____ system.
a. Thing
b. Coordinate0
c. Undefined
d. Undefined

124. In mathematics and its applications, a _____ is a system for assigning an n-tuple of numbers or scalars to each point in an n-dimensional space.
a. Coordinate system0
b. Concept
c. Undefined
d. Undefined

125. An _____ is when two lines intersect somewhere on a plane creating a right angle at intersection

Chapter 6. Inner Product Spaces

 a. Axes0
 b. Thing
 c. Undefined
 d. Undefined

126. In mathematics, an _____ .
 a. Thing
 b. Ellipse0
 c. Undefined
 d. Undefined

127. A _____ is the result of the addition of a set of numbers. The numbers may be natural numbers, complex numbers, matrices, or still more complicated objects. An infinite _____ is a subtle procedure known as a series.
 a. Sum0
 b. Thing
 c. Undefined
 d. Undefined

128. In mathematics, a _____ of a number x is a number r such that r^2 = x, or in words, a number r whose square (the result of multiplying the number by itself) is x.
 a. Square root0
 b. Thing
 c. Undefined
 d. Undefined

129. In mathematics, a _____ of a complex-valued function f is a member x of the domain of f such that f(x) vanishes at x, that is, x : f (x) = 0.
 a. Thing
 b. Root0
 c. Undefined
 d. Undefined

130. In logic, and especially in its applications to mathematics and philosophy, a _____ is an exception to a proposed general rule, i.e., a specific instance of the falsity of a universal quantification (a "for all" statement).

Chapter 6. Inner Product Spaces

    a. Thing
    b. Counterexample0
    c. Undefined
    d. Undefined

131. In mathematics, particularly linear algebra, two matrices A and B are said to be _____ if it is possible to transform A into B by a sequence of elementary operations.
    a. Equivalent matrices0
    b. Thing
    c. Undefined
    d. Undefined

132. An _____ is a binary relation between two elements of a set which groups them together as being equivalent in some way.
    a. Thing
    b. Equivalence relation0
    c. Undefined
    d. Undefined

133. An _____ is a square matrix which has an inverse.
    a. Invertible matrix0
    b. Thing
    c. Undefined
    d. Undefined

134. The _____, the average in everyday English, which is also called the arithmetic _____ (and is distinguished from the geometric _____ or harmonic _____). The average is also called the sample _____. The expected value of a random variable, which is also called the population _____.
    a. Thing
    b. Mean0
    c. Undefined
    d. Undefined

135. _____ is an algorithm which can be used to determine the solutions of a system of linear equations, to find the rank of a matrix, and to calculate the inverse of an invertible square matrix.

Chapter 6. Inner Product Spaces

a. Gaussian elimination0
b. Thing
c. Undefined
d. Undefined

136. In mathematics, the _____ (also nullspace) of an operator A is the set of all operands v which solve the equation Av = 0. It is also called the kernel of A.
a. Thing
b. Null space0
c. Undefined
d. Undefined

137. In mathematics, the _____ of a function is the set of all "output" values produced by that function. Given a function $f: A \to B$, the _____ of f, is defined to be the set $\{x \in B : x = f(a)$ for some $a \in A\}$.
a. Range0
b. Thing
c. Undefined
d. Undefined

138. In mathematics, the _____ functions are functions of an angle; they are important when studying triangles and modeling periodic phenomena, among many other applications.
a. Thing
b. Trigonometric0
c. Undefined
d. Undefined

139. _____ is a finite linear combination of sin and cos nx with n a natural number.
a. Thing
b. Trigonometric polynomial0
c. Undefined
d. Undefined

140. In mathematics and logic, a _____ proof is a way of showing the truth or falsehood of a given statement by a straightforward combination of established facts, usually existing lemmas and theorems, without making any further assumptions.

Chapter 6. Inner Product Spaces

   a. Direct0
   b. Thing
   c. Undefined
   d. Undefined

141. A _____ is a condition or value that is not limited to a specific set of values but can vary infinitely within a continuum.
   a. Spectrum0
   b. Thing
   c. Undefined
   d. Undefined

142. In mathematics, an _____ number is a complex number whose square is a negative real number. They were defined in 1572 by Rafael Bombelli.
   a. Thing
   b. Imaginary0
   c. Undefined
   d. Undefined

143. In mathematics, an _____ is something that does not change under a set of transformations. The property of being an _____ is invariance.
   a. Invariant0
   b. Thing
   c. Undefined
   d. Undefined

144. The _____ integers are all the integers from zero on upwards.
   a. Thing
   b. Nonnegative0
   c. Undefined
   d. Undefined

145. In common philosophical language, a proposition or _____, is the content of an assertion, that is, it is true-or-false and defined by the meaning of a particular piece of language.

Chapter 6. Inner Product Spaces

a. Concept
b. Statement0
c. Undefined
d. Undefined

146. _____ is a circle with a unit radius, i.e., a circle whose radius is 1.
a. Unit circle0
b. Thing
c. Undefined
d. Undefined

147. In Euclidean geometry, a _____ is the set of all points in a plane at a fixed distance, called the radius, from a given point, the center.
a. Circle0
b. Thing
c. Undefined
d. Undefined

148. In classical geometry, a _____ of a circle or sphere is any line segment from its center to its boundary. By extension, the _____ of a circle or sphere is the length of any such segment. The _____ is half the diameter. In science and engineering the term _____ of curvature is commonly used as a synonym for _____.
a. Radius0
b. Thing
c. Undefined
d. Undefined

149. An _____ is a straight line around which a geometric figure can be rotated.
a. Axis0
b. Thing
c. Undefined
d. Undefined

150. In linear algebra, a _____ of a matrix A is the determinant of some smaller square matrix, cut down from A.

Chapter 6. Inner Product Spaces

a. Minor0
b. Thing
c. Undefined
d. Undefined

151. In mathematics, _____ is the decomposition of an object into a product of other objects, or factors, which when multiplied together give the original.
a. Thing
b. Factoring0
c. Undefined
d. Undefined

152. _____ element of an element x with respect to a binary operation * with identity element e is an element y such that x * y = y * x = e. In particular,
a. Thing
b. Inverse0
c. Undefined
d. Undefined

153. In linear algebra, the _____ refers to a matrix consisting of the coefficients of the variables in a set of linear equations.
a. Coefficient matrix0
b. Thing
c. Undefined
d. Undefined

154. A _____ is a symbolic representation denoting a quantity or expression. It often represents an "unknown" quantity that has the potential to change.
a. Thing
b. Variable0
c. Undefined
d. Undefined

155. _____ is a mathematical subject that includes the study of limits, derivatives, integrals, and power series and constitutes a major part of modern university curriculum.

Chapter 6. Inner Product Spaces

  a. Calculus0
  b. Thing
  c. Undefined
  d. Undefined

156. In mathematics, a _____ on a vector space V over a field F is a mapping V × V → F which is linear in both arguments.
  a. Bilinear form0
  b. Thing
  c. Undefined
  d. Undefined

157. In mathematics, _____ is an elementary arithmetic operation. When one of the numbers is a whole number, _____ is the repeated sum of the other number.
  a. Thing
  b. Multiplication0
  c. Undefined
  d. Undefined

158. In mathematics, and in particular in abstract algebra, the _____ is a property of binary operations that generalises the distributive law from elementary algebra.
  a. Distributive property0
  b. Thing
  c. Undefined
  d. Undefined

159. In mathematics, an _____ (Greek:isos "equal", and morphe "shape") is a bijective map f such that both f and its inverse f^{-1} are homomorphisms, i.e. *structure-preserving* mappings.
  a. Thing
  b. Isomorphism0
  c. Undefined
  d. Undefined

160. As an abstract term, _____ means similarity between objects.

a. Congruence0
b. Thing
c. Undefined
d. Undefined

161. In geometry, two sets are called _____ if one can be transformed into the other by an isometry, i.e., a combination of translations, rotations and reflections.
a. Thing
b. Congruent0
c. Undefined
d. Undefined

162. In linear algebra, a _____ is a square matrix, A, that is equal to its transpose.
a. Thing
b. Symmetric Matrix0
c. Undefined
d. Undefined

163. In mathematics and physics, a _____ associates a scalar value, which can be either mathematical in definition, or physical, to every point in space.
a. Thing
b. Scalar field0
c. Undefined
d. Undefined

164. Elementary _____ are simple transformations which can be applied to a matrix without changing the linear system of equations that it represents.
a. Row operations0
b. Thing
c. Undefined
d. Undefined

165. In mathematics, computing, linguistics, and related disciplines, an _____ is a finite list of well-defined instructions for accomplishing some task which, given an initial state, will terminate in a defined end-state.

Chapter 6. Inner Product Spaces

a. Concept
b. Algorithm0
c. Undefined
d. Undefined

166. An _____ is a combination of numbers, operators, grouping symbols and/or free variables and bound variables arranged in a meaningful way which can be evaluated..
a. Thing
b. Expression0
c. Undefined
d. Undefined

167. _____ is a quadric, a type of surface in three dimensions
a. Thing
b. Elliptic paraboloid0
c. Undefined
d. Undefined

168. _____ is a quadric
a. Thing
b. Paraboloid0
c. Undefined
d. Undefined

169. _____ is a point on the domain of a function
a. Critical point0
b. Thing
c. Undefined
d. Undefined

170. In mathematics, maxima and minima, known collectively as extrema, are the largest value maximum or smallest value minimum, that a function takes in a point either within a given neighborhood local _____ or on the function domain in its entirety global _____.

a. Extremum0
b. Thing
c. Undefined
d. Undefined

171. A real-valued function f defined on the real line is said to have a _____ point at the point x∗, if there exists some ε > 0, such that f when x − x∗ < ε.
a. Thing
b. Local maximum0
c. Undefined
d. Undefined

172. Acid _____ ratio measures the ability of a company to use its near cash or quick assets to immediately extinguish its current liabilities.
a. Test0
b. Thing
c. Undefined
d. Undefined

173. _____ determines whether a given stationary point of a function is a maximum or a minimum.
a. Thing
b. Second derivative test0
c. Undefined
d. Undefined

174. Mathematical _____ are the wide variety of ways to capture an abstract mathematical concept or relationship.
a. Representations0
b. Thing
c. Undefined
d. Undefined

175. The word _____ is used in a variety of ways in mathematics.

Chapter 6. Inner Product Spaces

a. Thing
b. Index0
c. Undefined
d. Undefined

176. In the scientific method, an _____ (Latin: ex-+-periri, "of (or from) trying"), is a set of actions and observations, performed in the context of solving a particular problem or question, in order to support or falsify a hypothesis or research concerning phenomena.
a. Thing
b. Experiment0
c. Undefined
d. Undefined

177. _____ is electromagnetic radiation with a wavelength that is visible to the eye (visible _____) or, in a technical or scientific context, electromagnetic radiation of any wavelength.
a. Light0
b. Thing
c. Undefined
d. Undefined

178. A _____ is a unit of length, usually used to measure distance, in a number of different systems, including Imperial units, United States customary units and Norwegian/Swedish mil. Its size can vary from system to system, but in each is between 1 and 10 kilometers. In contemporary English contexts _____ refers to either:
a. Thing
b. Mile0
c. Undefined
d. Undefined

179. _____ (March 14, 1879 - April 18, 1955) was a German-born theoretical physicist who is best known for his theory of relativity and specifically mass-energy equivalence, $E = mc^2$.
a. Albert Einstein0
b. Person
c. Undefined
d. Undefined

180. _____ is the transport of people on a trip/journey or the process or time involved in a person or object moving from one location to another.
   a. Travel0
   b. Thing
   c. Undefined
   d. Undefined

181. _____ of an object is its speed in a particular direction.
   a. Thing
   b. Velocity0
   c. Undefined
   d. Undefined

182. An _____ is any starting assumption from which other statements are logically derived
   a. Thing
   b. Axiom0
   c. Undefined
   d. Undefined

183. The _____ in a vacuum is an important physical constant denoted by the letter c for constant or the Latin word celeritas meaning "swiftness
   a. Thing
   b. Speed of light0
   c. Undefined
   d. Undefined

184. In a mathematical proof or a syllogism, a _____ is a statement that is the logical consequence of preceding statements.
   a. Conclusion0
   b. Concept
   c. Undefined
   d. Undefined

185. The _____ of measurement are a globally standardized and modernized form of the metric system.

Chapter 6. Inner Product Spaces

   a. Units0
   b. Thing
   c. Undefined
   d. Undefined

186. In _____ algebra, a *-ring is an associative ring with an antilinear, antiautomorphism * : A ¨ A which is an involution.
   a. Thing
   b. Star0
   c. Undefined
   d. Undefined

187. A _____ is a deliberate process for transforming one or more inputs into one or more results.
   a. Thing
   b. Calculation0
   c. Undefined
   d. Undefined

188. In set theory and other branches of mathematics, the _____ of a collection of sets is the set that contains everything that belongs to any of the sets, but nothing else.
   a. Thing
   b. Union0
   c. Undefined
   d. Undefined

189. In mathematics, two sets are said to be _____ if they have no element in common. For example, {1, 2, 3} and {4, 5, 6} are sets which are _____.
   a. Disjoint0
   b. Thing
   c. Undefined
   d. Undefined

Chapter 7. Canonical Forms

1. In mathematics, a _____ number is a number which can be expressed as a ratio of two integers. Non-integer _____ numbers (commonly called fractions) are usually written as the vulgar fraction a / b, where b is not zero.
   a. Rational0
   b. Thing
   c. Undefined
   d. Undefined

2. The word _____ comes from the Latin word linearis, which means created by lines.
   a. Thing
   b. Linear0
   c. Undefined
   d. Undefined

3. In mathematics, a _____ is an expression that is constructed from one or more variables and constants, using only the operations of addition, subtraction, multiplication, and constant positive whole number exponents. is a _____. Note in particular that division by an expression containing a variable is not in general allowed in polynomials. [1]
   a. Polynomial0
   b. Thing
   c. Undefined
   d. Undefined

4. Generally, in mathematics, a _____ of an object is a standard presentation.
   a. Thing
   b. Canonical form0
   c. Undefined
   d. Undefined

5. In linear algebra, a square matrix A is called _____ if it is similar to a diagonal matrix, i.e. if there exists an invertible matrix P such that P â˜'1AP is a diagonal matrix. If V is a finite-dimensional vector space, then a linear map T : V â†' V is called _____ if there exists a basis of V with respect to which T is represented by a diagonal matrix. Diagonalization is the process of finding a corresponding diagonal matrix for a _____ matrix or linear map.
   a. Thing
   b. Diagonalizable0
   c. Undefined
   d. Undefined

Chapter 7. Canonical Forms

6. In mathematics, _____ is the decomposition of an object into a product of other objects, or factors, which when multiplied together give the original.
   a. Factoring0
   b. Thing
   c. Undefined
   d. Undefined

7. In set theory and other branches of mathematics, the _____ of a collection of sets is the set that contains everything that belongs to any of the sets, but nothing else.
   a. Union0
   b. Thing
   c. Undefined
   d. Undefined

8. An _____ of a given transformation is the set of all eigenvectors of that transformation that have the same eigenvalue, together with the zero vector (which has no direction). An _____ is an example of a subspace of a vector space.
   a. Thing
   b. Eigenspace0
   c. Undefined
   d. Undefined

9. The _____, the average in everyday English, which is also called the arithmetic _____ (and is distinguished from the geometric _____ or harmonic _____). The average is also called the sample _____. The expected value of a random variable, which is also called the population _____.
   a. Thing
   b. Mean0
   c. Undefined
   d. Undefined

10. The _____ of a ring R is defined to be the smallest positive integer n such that $n\,a = 0$, for all a in R.
    a. Thing
    b. Characteristic0
    c. Undefined
    d. Undefined

Chapter 7. Canonical Forms

11. In physics and in _____ calculus, a spatial _____, or simply _____, is a concept characterized by a magnitude and a direction.
   a. Vector0
   b. Thing
   c. Undefined
   d. Undefined

12. _____ is a collection of objects called vectors that, informally speaking, may be scaled and added.
   a. Thing
   b. Vector space0
   c. Undefined
   d. Undefined

13. _____ is a set, with some particular properties and usually some additional structure, such as the operations of addition or multiplication, for instance.
   a. Thing
   b. Space0
   c. Undefined
   d. Undefined

14. In linear algebra, real numbers are called scalars and relate to vectors in a vector space through the operation of _____ multiplication, in which a vector can be multiplied by a number to produce another vector.
   a. Thing
   b. Scalar0
   c. Undefined
   d. Undefined

15. A vector can be thought of as an arrow. It has a length, called its magnitude, and it points in some particular direction. A linear transformation inputs a vector and changes it, usually changing both its magnitude and its direction. An eigenvector of a given linear transformation is a vector which is simply multiplied by a constant called the _____ during that transformation.
   a. Eigenvalue0
   b. Thing
   c. Undefined
   d. Undefined

Chapter 7. Canonical Forms

16. An _____ of a linear transformation is a non-zero vector that is either left unaffected or simply multiplied by a scale factor after the transformation.
   a. Thing
   b. Eigenvector0
   c. Undefined
   d. Undefined

17. A _____ is a set whose members are members of another set or a set contained within another set.
   a. Subset0
   b. Thing
   c. Undefined
   d. Undefined

18. In linear algebra and related areas of mathematics, the null vector or _____ is the vector in Euclidean space, all of whose components are zero.
   a. Thing
   b. Zero vector0
   c. Undefined
   d. Undefined

19. In mathematics, a _____ is a countable collection of open covers of a topological space that satisfies certain separation axioms.
   a. Development0
   b. Thing
   c. Undefined
   d. Undefined

20. In mathematics, a _____ is a statement that can be proved on the basis of explicitly stated or previously agreed assumptions.
   a. Thing
   b. Theorem0
   c. Undefined
   d. Undefined

21. In mathematics, _____ is an elementary arithmetic operation. When one of the numbers is a whole number, _____ is the repeated sum of the other number.

146 Chapter 7. Canonical Forms

a. Multiplication0
b. Thing
c. Undefined
d. Undefined

22. In mathematics, a _____ is a demonstration that, assuming certain axioms, some statement is necessarily true.
a. Proof0
b. Thing
c. Undefined
d. Undefined

23. _____ is one of the basic operations defining a vector space in linear algebra.
a. Thing
b. Scalar multiplication0
c. Undefined
d. Undefined

24. In mathematics, a set is called _____ if there is a bijection between the set and some set of the form {1, 2, ..., n} where n is a natural number.
a. Thing
b. Finite0
c. Undefined
d. Undefined

25. The _____ of a member of a multiset is how many memberships in the multiset it has.
a. Multiplicity0
b. Thing
c. Undefined
d. Undefined

26. In mathematics, a _____ of an integer n, also called a factor of n, is an integer which evenly divides n without leaving a remainder.

a. Thing
b. Divisor0
c. Undefined
d. Undefined

27. A _____, is a symbolized depiction of space which highlights relations between components of that space. Most usually a _____ is a two-dimensional, geometrically accurate representation of a three-dimensional space.
   a. Map0
   b. Thing
   c. Undefined
   d. Undefined

28. A _____ consists either of a suggested explanation for a phenomenon or of a reasoned proposal suggesting a possible correlation between multiple phenomena.
   a. Hypothesis0
   b. Thing
   c. Undefined
   d. Undefined

29. In combinatorial mathematics, a _____ is an un-ordered collection of unique elements.
   a. Concept
   b. Combination0
   c. Undefined
   d. Undefined

30. Mathematical _____ is used to represent ideas.
   a. Thing
   b. Notation0
   c. Undefined
   d. Undefined

31. In mathematics, two sets are said to be _____ if they have no element in common. For example, {1, 2, 3} and {4, 5, 6} are sets which are _____.

148   Chapter 7. Canonical Forms

   a. Disjoint0
   b. Thing
   c. Undefined
   d. Undefined

32. In mathematics, an _____ is a theorem with a statement beginning 'there exist ...'. That is, in more formal terms of symbolic logic, it is a theorem with a statement involving the existential quantifier.
   a. Thing
   b. Existence theorem0
   c. Undefined
   d. Undefined

33. _____ is a method of mathematical proof typically used to establish that a given statement is true of all natural numbers
   a. Thing
   b. Mathematical induction0
   c. Undefined
   d. Undefined

34. Initial objects are also called _____, and terminal objects are also called final.
   a. Coterminal0
   b. Thing
   c. Undefined
   d. Undefined

35. In common philosophical language, a proposition or _____, is the content of an assertion, that is, it is true-or-false and defined by the meaning of a particular piece of language.
   a. Statement0
   b. Concept
   c. Undefined
   d. Undefined

36. In mathematics, an _____ is a statement about the relative size or order of two objects.

Chapter 7. Canonical Forms

a. Thing
b. Inequality0
c. Undefined
d. Undefined

37. A _____ is a mathematical statement which follows easily from a previously proven statement, typically a mathematical theorem.
a. Thing
b. Corollary0
c. Undefined
d. Undefined

38. In mathematics, a _____ is a rectangular table of numbers or, more generally, a table consisting of abstract quantities that can be added and multiplied.
a. Thing
b. Matrix0
c. Undefined
d. Undefined

39. In mathematics, a matrix can be thought of as each row or _____ being a vector. Hence, a space formed by row vectors or _____ vectors are said to be a row space or a _____ space.
a. Concept
b. Column0
c. Undefined
d. Undefined

40. Deductive _____ is the kind of _____ in which the conclusion is necessitated by, or reached from, previously known facts (the premises).
a. Thing
b. Reasoning0
c. Undefined
d. Undefined

41. A _____ is the result of the addition of a set of numbers. The numbers may be natural numbers, complex numbers, matrices, or still more complicated objects. An infinite _____ is a subtle procedure known as a series.

a. Thing
b. Sum0
c. Undefined
d. Undefined

42. In mathematics and logic, a _____ proof is a way of showing the truth or falsehood of a given statement by a straightforward combination of established facts, usually existing lemmas and theorems, without making any further assumptions.
a. Thing
b. Direct0
c. Undefined
d. Undefined

43. Acid _____ ratio measures the ability of a company to use its near cash or quick assets to immediately extinguish its current liabilities.
a. Test0
b. Thing
c. Undefined
d. Undefined

44. The easiest _____ prime numbers resides in the use of the Sieve of Eratosthenes, an algorithm that discovers all prime numbers to a specified integer.
a. Method for finding0
b. Thing
c. Undefined
d. Undefined

45. In computer science an _____ is a data structure that consists of a group of elements having a single name that are accessed by indexing. In most programming languages each element has the same data type and the _____ occupies a continuous area of storage.
a. Thing
b. Array0
c. Undefined
d. Undefined

Chapter 7. Canonical Forms

46. A _____ is a simplified and structured visual representation of concepts, ideas, constructions, relations, statistical data, anatomy etc used in all aspects of human activities to visualize and clarify the topic.
   a. Diagram0
   b. Thing
   c. Undefined
   d. Undefined

47. _____ is the mathematical action of repeatedly adding or subtracting one, usually to find out how many objects there are or to set aside a desired number of objects.
   a. Thing
   b. Counting0
   c. Undefined
   d. Undefined

48. Mathematical _____ are demonstrations that,assuming certain axioms, some statement is necessarily true.
   a. Proofs0
   b. Thing
   c. Undefined
   d. Undefined

49. In mathematics, an _____ is something that does not change under a set of transformations. The property of being an _____ is invariance.
   a. Invariant0
   b. Thing
   c. Undefined
   d. Undefined

50. _____ the expected value of a random variable displays the average or central value of the variable.It is a summary value of the distribution of the variable.
   a. Thing
   b. Determining0
   c. Undefined
   d. Undefined

51. In mathematics, the _____ (also nullspace) of an operator A is the set of all operands v which solve the equation Av = 0. It is also called the kernel of A.

a. Null space0
b. Thing
c. Undefined
d. Undefined

52. A _____ is an equation in which each term is either a constant or the product of a constant times the first power of a variable.
   a. Linear equation0
   b. Thing
   c. Undefined
   d. Undefined

53. A _____ is a deliberate process for transforming one or more inputs into one or more results.
   a. Thing
   b. Calculation0
   c. Undefined
   d. Undefined

54. A _____ is a symbolic representation denoting a quantity or expression. It often represents an "unknown" quantity that has the potential to change.
   a. Variable0
   b. Thing
   c. Undefined
   d. Undefined

55. In mathematics, there are several meanings of _____ depending on the subject.
   a. Thing
   b. Degree0
   c. Undefined
   d. Undefined

56. The mathematical concept of a _____ expresses the intuitive idea of deterministic dependence between two quantities, one of which is viewed as primary and the other as secondary. A _____ then is a way to associate a unique output for each input of a specified type, for example, a real number or an element of a given set.

Chapter 7. Canonical Forms

　　a. Thing
　　b. Function0
　　c. Undefined
　　d. Undefined

57. In mathematics, a _____ is a condition that a solution to an optimization problem must satisfy in order to be acceptable.
　　a. Constraint0
　　b. Thing
　　c. Undefined
　　d. Undefined

58. Order theory is a branch of mathematics that studies various kinds of binary relations that capture the intuitive notion of a mathematical _____.
　　a. Ordering0
　　b. Thing
　　c. Undefined
　　d. Undefined

59. A _____ can refer to a line joining two nonadjacent vertices of a polygon or polyhedron, or in some contexts any upward or downward sloping line. .
　　a. Diagonal0
　　b. Thing
　　c. Undefined
　　d. Undefined

60. _____ is a square matrix in which the entries outside the main diagonal are all zero.
　　a. Diagonal matrix0
　　b. Thing
　　c. Undefined
　　d. Undefined

61. In mathematics, the idea of _____ generalises the concepts of negation, in relation to addition, and reciprocal, in relation to multiplication.

Chapter 7. Canonical Forms

a. Inverse element0
b. Thing
c. Undefined
d. Undefined

62. An _____ is a square matrix which has an inverse.
a. Invertible matrix0
b. Thing
c. Undefined
d. Undefined

63. In mathematics, an element x of a ring R is called _____ if there exists some positive integer n such that $x^n = 0$.
a. Nilpotent0
b. Thing
c. Undefined
d. Undefined

64. _____ is a special kind of square matrix where the entries below or above the main diagonal are zero.
a. Triangular form0
b. Thing
c. Undefined
d. Undefined

65. In plane geometry, a _____ is a polygon with four equal sides, four right angles, and parallel opposite sides. In algebra, the _____ of a number is that number multiplied by itself.
a. Thing
b. Square0
c. Undefined
d. Undefined

66. In mathematics, a _____ is an ordered list of objects. Like a set, it contains members, also called elements or terms, and the number of terms is called the length of the _____. Unlike a set, order matters, and the exact same elements can appear multiple times at different positions in the _____.

Chapter 7. Canonical Forms

a. Thing
b. Sequence0
c. Undefined
d. Undefined

67. _____ Logic is a concept in traditional logic referring to a "type of immediate inference in which from a given proposition another proposition is inferred which has as its subject the predicate of the original proposition and as its predicate the subject of the original proposition (the quality of the proposition being retained)."
a. Concept
b. Converse0
c. Undefined
d. Undefined

68. In mathematics, a _____ describes the transitions of a Markov chain. It has found use in probability theory, statistics and linear algebra, as well as computer science.
a. Thing
b. Stochastic matrix0
c. Undefined
d. Undefined

69. In mathematics, a _____ is a constant multiplicative factor of a certain object. The object can be such things as a variable, a vector, a function, etc. For example, the _____ of $9x^2$ is 9.
a. Coefficient0
b. Thing
c. Undefined
d. Undefined

70. The _____ is a measurement of how a function changes when the values of its inputs change.
a. Thing
b. Derivative0
c. Undefined
d. Undefined

71. In mathematics, an inequality is a statement about the relative size or order of two objects. For example 14 > 10, or 14 is _____ 10.

Chapter 7. Canonical Forms

  a. Thing
  b. Greater than0
  c. Undefined
  d. Undefined

72. In mathematics, factorization (British English: factorisation) or factoring is the decomposition of an object (for example, a number, a polynomial, or a matrix) into a product of other objects, or _____, which when multiplied together give the original.
  a. Thing
  b. Factors0
  c. Undefined
  d. Undefined

73. A _____ is traditionally an infinitesimally small change in a variable.
  a. Differential0
  b. Thing
  c. Undefined
  d. Undefined

74. _____, a field in mathematics, is the study of how functions change when their inputs change. The primary object of study in _____ is the derivative.
  a. Thing
  b. Differential calculus0
  c. Undefined
  d. Undefined

75. _____ is an operator defined as a function of the _____.
  a. Thing
  b. Differentiation operator0
  c. Undefined
  d. Undefined

76. The _____ are the only integral domain whose positive elements are well-ordered, and in which order is preserved by addition. Like the natural numbers, the _____ form a countably infinite set. The set of all _____ is usually denoted in mathematics by a boldface Z .

a. Integers0
b. Thing
c. Undefined
d. Undefined

77. Mathematical _____ are the wide variety of ways to capture an abstract mathematical concept or relationship.
a. Thing
b. Representations0
c. Undefined
d. Undefined

78. _____ is the fee paid on borrowed money.
a. Interest0
b. Thing
c. Undefined
d. Undefined

79. _____ has many meanings, most of which simply .
a. Thing
b. Power0
c. Undefined
d. Undefined

80. Vacuous truth is a special topic of first-order logic. A conditional assertion is _____ if the assertion can already be shown to be true and the condition is logically unrelated to the assertion.
a. Vacuously true0
b. Thing
c. Undefined
d. Undefined

81. A _____ fraction is a fraction in which the absolute value of the numerator is less than the denominator--hence, the absolute value of the fraction is less than 1.

Chapter 7. Canonical Forms

a. Thing
b. Proper0
c. Undefined
d. Undefined

82. In mathematics, a _____ is the result of multiplying, or an expression that identifies factors to be multiplied.
a. Product0
b. Thing
c. Undefined
d. Undefined

83. _____ is the rearrangement of objects or symbols into distinguishable sequences.
a. Thing
b. Permutation0
c. Undefined
d. Undefined

84. _____ is a concept that occurs in ring theory, a branch of mathematics.
a. Annihilator0
b. Thing
c. Undefined
d. Undefined

85. An _____ is a combination of numbers, operators, grouping symbols and/or free variables and bound variables arranged in a meaningful way which can be evaluated..
a. Expression0
b. Thing
c. Undefined
d. Undefined

86. _____ refers to the reduction of the body of a formerly living organism into simpler forms of matter.

a. Thing
b. Decomposing0
c. Undefined
d. Undefined

Chapter 1

1. a	2. a	3. a	4. a	5. a	6. b	7. a	8. a	9. a	10. a
11. a	12. b	13. a	14. a	15. a	16. a	17. b	18. b	19. b	20. a
21. b	22. a	23. a	24. a	25. b	26. a	27. b	28. b	29. b	30. a
31. a	32. b	33. b	34. b	35. a	36. b	37. a	38. a	39. a	40. a
41. a	42. a	43. b	44. b	45. a	46. b	47. a	48. a	49. b	50. b
51. b	52. a	53. b	54. a	55. a	56. b	57. b	58. b	59. a	60. b
61. a	62. b	63. b	64. a	65. a	66. a	67. a	68. b	69. b	70. a
71. b	72. b	73. a	74. a	75. a	76. a	77. a	78. a	79. b	80. a
81. b	82. b	83. a	84. a	85. b	86. b	87. b	88. a	89. b	90. a
91. a	92. a	93. a	94. a	95. b	96. b	97. b	98. a	99. b	100. b
101. b	102. a	103. a	104. a	105. b	106. a	107. a	108. b	109. b	110. a
111. a	112. a	113. b	114. a	115. a	116. b				

Chapter 2

1. b	2. a	3. b	4. b	5. b	6. b	7. b	8. a	9. b	10. a
11. a	12. a	13. b	14. b	15. b	16. a	17. a	18. a	19. a	20. a
21. a	22. a	23. b	24. b	25. a	26. b	27. a	28. a	29. a	30. a
31. a	32. a	33. a	34. b	35. a	36. b	37. b	38. b	39. b	40. a
41. a	42. a	43. a	44. a	45. b	46. b	47. a	48. b	49. a	50. a
51. b	52. b	53. b	54. a	55. b	56. a	57. b	58. a	59. a	60. a
61. b	62. a	63. a	64. b	65. a	66. b	67. a	68. a	69. b	70. b
71. a	72. a	73. a	74. b	75. a	76. a	77. a	78. a	79. b	80. a
81. a	82. a	83. b	84. b	85. b	86. a	87. b	88. a	89. a	90. b
91. a	92. a	93. a	94. a	95. a	96. a	97. a	98. b	99. a	100. a
101. a	102. b	103. b	104. b	105. b	106. a	107. a	108. b	109. b	110. a
111. a	112. a	113. b	114. a	115. b	116. a	117. b	118. b	119. a	120. a
121. b	122. b	123. b	124. a	125. a	126. a	127. a	128. a		

Chapter 3

1. b	2. a	3. b	4. a	5. b	6. b	7. a	8. b	9. a	10. a
11. a	12. a	13. b	14. a	15. a	16. a	17. a	18. a	19. a	20. a
21. a	22. b	23. a	24. a	25. b	26. a	27. b	28. b	29. a	30. b
31. b	32. b	33. b	34. a	35. a	36. b	37. b	38. a	39. b	40. b
41. b	42. a	43. a	44. a	45. a	46. a	47. a	48. b	49. b	50. a
51. b	52. a	53. b	54. b	55. a	56. b	57. a	58. a	59. b	60. a
61. a	62. b	63. a	64. b	65. b	66. b	67. b	68. b	69. b	70. b
71. b	72. a	73. a	74. a						

ANSWER KEY

Chapter 4

1. b	2. a	3. a	4. b	5. b	6. b	7. a	8. a	9. a	10. a
11. a	12. b	13. b	14. b	15. a	16. a	17. a	18. b	19. b	20. a
21. a	22. b	23. a	24. a	25. a	26. b	27. a	28. b	29. a	30. b
31. b	32. a	33. b	34. a	35. a	36. b	37. a	38. b	39. b	40. a
41. a	42. a	43. a	44. a	45. b	46. b	47. a	48. a	49. b	50. a
51. a	52. a	53. b	54. a	55. b	56. a	57. a	58. a	59. b	60. b
61. b	62. a	63. a	64. b	65. b	66. b	67. b	68. a	69. b	

Chapter 5

1. b	2. a	3. a	4. b	5. b	6. a	7. a	8. b	9. a	10. a
11. b	12. b	13. a	14. a	15. a	16. b	17. b	18. b	19. a	20. b
21. b	22. b	23. b	24. b	25. b	26. b	27. b	28. b	29. a	30. a
31. a	32. a	33. a	34. b	35. a	36. a	37. b	38. b	39. a	40. a
41. a	42. b	43. a	44. b	45. b	46. b	47. b	48. b	49. a	50. a
51. a	52. a	53. b	54. b	55. b	56. b	57. a	58. a	59. b	60. b
61. b	62. a	63. a	64. b	65. b	66. b	67. b	68. b	69. b	70. b
71. b	72. b	73. b	74. b	75. a	76. b	77. b	78. b	79. b	80. b
81. a	82. a	83. a	84. a	85. a	86. b	87. a	88. a	89. a	90. a
91. b	92. a	93. b	94. a	95. a	96. a	97. a	98. b	99. a	100. b
101. a	102. b	103. a	104. b	105. a	106. a	107. a	108. b	109. b	110. a
111. b	112. b	113. a	114. b	115. a	116. a	117. a	118. b	119. a	

Chapter 6

1. b	2. b	3. a	4. a	5. a	6. b	7. a	8. a	9. a	10. b
11. b	12. b	13. b	14. a	15. b	16. a	17. a	18. a	19. b	20. a
21. a	22. b	23. a	24. a	25. b	26. b	27. b	28. b	29. a	30. a
31. b	32. a	33. b	34. b	35. a	36. a	37. a	38. a	39. a	40. a
41. b	42. b	43. a	44. b	45. a	46. b	47. b	48. a	49. b	50. b
51. a	52. a	53. b	54. a	55. b	56. b	57. a	58. a	59. b	60. b
61. a	62. a	63. a	64. a	65. b	66. b	67. b	68. a	69. b	70. a
71. b	72. a	73. a	74. b	75. a	76. b	77. a	78. a	79. a	80. a
81. a	82. a	83. a	84. b	85. a	86. a	87. b	88. a	89. b	90. b
91. a	92. b	93. a	94. b	95. b	96. a	97. b	98. b	99. b	100. a
101. b	102. a	103. b	104. a	105. a	106. a	107. a	108. a	109. b	110. b
111. b	112. a	113. b	114. b	115. a	116. a	117. a	118. a	119. a	120. a
121. a	122. a	123. b	124. a	125. a	126. b	127. a	128. a	129. b	130. b
131. a	132. b	133. a	134. b	135. a	136. b	137. a	138. b	139. b	140. a
141. a	142. b	143. a	144. b	145. b	146. a	147. a	148. a	149. a	150. a
151. b	152. b	153. a	154. b	155. a	156. a	157. b	158. a	159. b	160. a
161. b	162. b	163. b	164. a	165. b	166. b	167. b	168. b	169. a	170. a
171. b	172. a	173. b	174. a	175. b	176. b	177. a	178. b	179. a	180. a
181. b	182. b	183. b	184. a	185. a	186. b	187. b	188. b	189. a	

Chapter 7

1. a	2. b	3. a	4. b	5. b	6. a	7. a	8. b	9. b	10. b
11. a	12. b	13. b	14. b	15. a	16. b	17. a	18. b	19. a	20. b
21. a	22. a	23. b	24. b	25. a	26. b	27. a	28. a	29. b	30. b
31. a	32. b	33. b	34. a	35. a	36. b	37. b	38. b	39. b	40. b
41. b	42. b	43. a	44. a	45. b	46. a	47. b	48. a	49. a	50. b
51. a	52. a	53. b	54. a	55. b	56. b	57. a	58. a	59. a	60. a
61. a	62. a	63. a	64. a	65. b	66. b	67. b	68. b	69. a	70. b
71. b	72. b	73. a	74. b	75. b	76. a	77. b	78. a	79. b	80. a
81. b	82. a	83. b	84. a	85. a	86. b				